WILD AND TEMPERATE SEAS

50 Favourite UK Dives

Will Appleyard

With Kirsty Andrews, Dan Bolt, Jason Brown, Jake Davies, Alex Gibson, Stuart Philpott and Elaine Whiteford

ISBN 978-1-909455-34-4 (Paperback)
ISBN 978-1-909455-35-1 (EPUB ebook)
ISBN 978-1-909455-36-8 (PDF ebook)

Cataloguing-In-Publication Data A catalogue record for this book can be obtained from the British Library.

Copyright © 2020 Will Appleyard et al.
All intellectual property and associated rights are hereby asserted and reserved by the authors in full compliance with UK, European and international law. No part of this book may be copied, reproduced, stored in any retrieval system or transmitted in any form or by any means, including in hard copy or via the internet, without the prior written permission of the publishers to whom all such rights have been assigned worldwide.

Cover Design © 2020 Dived Up.
Cover photographs by Jason Brown.

Printed by Cambrian Printers, Aberystwyth.

Published 2020 by

Dived Up Publications
Oxford • United Kingdom
Email info@divedup.com
Web DivedUp.com

Contents

MAP 7
ACKNOWLEDGEMENTS 8
DIVEMASTER'S BRIEFING 9
INTRODUCTION 11

DORSET 14
by Will Appleyard

    Swanage Pier 16
    SS Kyarra 18
    MV Aeolian Sky 20
    HMS M2 22
    Chesil Cove 24
    Fact file 26

TORBAY 28
by Dan Bolt

    Babbacombe 30
    Beacon Cove 32
    Flat Rock 34
    London Bridge 36
    Meadfoot 38
    Shoalstone 40
    Fact file 42

PLYMOUTH 44
by Will Appleyard

    SS James Eagan Layne 46
    Eddystone Lighthouse 48
    Hatt Rock 50
    Blue Sharks (Snorkel) 52
    Fact file 54

PORTHKERRIS 56
by Will Appleyard

    Drawna Rocks 58
    Manacles Reefs 60
    SS Mohegan 62
    Fact file 64

ROCK 66
by Stuart Philpott

- SS Anna Sofie 68
- SS Sphene 70
- Fact file 72

LUNDY ISLAND 74
by Will Appleyard

- Gannets' Bay 76
- MV Robert 78
- Fact file 80

LLŶN PENINSULA 82
by Jake Davies and Will Appleyard

- Porth Ysgaden 84
- Criccieth Breakwater 86
- Gimblet Rock 88
- Porthdinllaen (Seagrass Meadow) 90
- Fact file 92

RATHLIN ISLAND 94
by Alex Gibson

- North Wall 96
- SS Lochgarry 98
- Fact file 100

FARNE ISLANDS 102
by Kirsty Andrews

- Seals 104
- Fact file 106

ST ABBS 108
by Elaine Whiteford

- Anemone Gullies 110
- Black Carr 112
- The Craig 114
- Fact file 116

LOCH LONG 118
by Elaine Whiteford

    Finnart (aka The A Frames) 120
    Twin Piers 122
    Fact file 124

LOCH FYNE 126
by Elaine Whiteford

    St Catherines (former Council Yard) 128
    Seal Reef 130
    Anchor Point 132
    Fact file 134

MULL 136
by Kirsty Andrews and Dan Bolt

    SS Hispania 138
    SS Rondo 140
    SS Shuna 142
    Fingal's Cave (Snorkel) 144
    Fact file 146

SCAPA FLOW 148
by Jason Brown

    SMS Brummer 150
    SMS Cöln 152
    SMS Dresden 154
    SMS Karlsruhe 156
    SMS König 158
    SMS Kronprinz Wilhelm 160
    SMS Markgraf 162
    Fact file 164

NORTH RONA AND SULA SGEIR 166
by Kirsty Andrews

    North Rona 168
    Sula Sgeir 170
    Fact file 172

THE AUTHOR AND CONTRIBUTORS 174

Acknowledgements

The author and contributors would like to thank the following people:

WILL. My inspirational Dad Steve Appleyard, Alex Gibson, divers Ana Rancaño, Rob Roslyn, Alyson Turner, Damian Brown, Tim Mountjoy and Helen Phillips, Dan Bolt, Elaine Whiteford, Jake Davies, Jason Brown, Kirsty Andrews, Stuart Philpott, the team @ O'Three for their continued support, Dale Spree @ Dive Beyond, Izzy @ Underwater Explorers Dorset, Ben & James @ In Deep Diving Plymouth, Steve Weinman, super skipper Dave Brown, Porthkerris Divers Cornwall, Divers Down Swanage, Bryan Jones, Matt @ Aerial Cornwall, Mike Deaton, INON UK, those that campaign to protect our seas, oceans and wild places and the kind folk who find the time to reply when I reach out.

ELAINE. Thanks to my husband, Mish, for his years of patient surface support.

JASON. Helen Hadley, skipper of MV Valkyrie, Hazel Weaver, skipper of MV Valhalla, Emily Turton, skipper of MV Huskyan, John Womack @ Otter Drysuits, Graham Blackmore at GUE, James Hall @ Sea&Sea UK, James Sanderson and Dean Martin @ Apeks UK, Martin and Amy Stanton @ Vobster Quay, Brett Thorpe @ Nautilus UK, Rufus, Rey and Tala for moral support, Georgina Brown.

KIRSTY. Bob, Malc, Bodie, Micky, Danny and all the other great skippers out there helping divers see the best of UK waters.

JAKE. The team @ O'Three, Suunto Dive and GoPro UK.

ALEX. Jan Gibson, Richard Lafferty, Paul Colley, Steve and Lisa @ INON UK, Stuart Allen, Henry Standing, Chris Stevens and Connor Slamon.

DAN. All my patient dive buddies over the years, my wife Anne (who, even as a non-diver, now knows more about UK marine life than many divers do!) and the members of the Devon Society of Underwater Photographers (DSoUP) for their constant inspiration and high-spirited companionship.

STUART. Swanage Boat Charters, Scimitar Diving, Harlyn Dive School, Steve Hutchinson (Hutch), Andrew Ricks and Becky Gill.

Divemaster's Briefing

The information in this book is provided to the best of our knowledge from details available at the time of publication. The marine environment is active and evolving — things can and do change. In most cases we have managed to obtain site marks directly from local skippers and although we cannot guarantee exact positioning in all cases, we believe the points given to be correct. We highly recommend supplementing the information in this guide with local advice should you choose to independently dive any of these sites. Certainly that is the case if you do not have the necessary training and experience to run a dive.

Alternatively, support the UK's dedicated band of professionals and enjoy a relaxing day instead. Most operators can offer guided or unguided diving, both from the shore and boats. Many charters operate almost as water taxi plus surface cover/safety provider. Those more used to full service diving in tropical locations may find this a bit different at first, but most soon enjoy the liberation of only needing to concern themselves with listening intently to the dive briefing, tracking the location of their buddy and making the decision over who should launch a surface marker buoy at the end of the dive.

Certain skills can be deemed essential for UK diving, including compass navigation, delayed surface marker buoy (DSMB) launch and management, and drysuit diving. Instruction on how to use this equipment is available from all of the diving agencies operating in the UK — it often forms part of the core diver training syllabus, or add-on courses are available.

Our beloved wrecks are never to be considered eternal time capsules, their form slowly degrading over time with the action of the sea and its salinity. The destinations themselves should never disappear however, and we hope that their biodiversity actually increases, rather than diminishes. We have done our best within this book to list the companies that we have used to transport us to the dive sites featured, to fill our tanks or both. Yet, boat charters and air stations from time to time change hands or sadly cease to trade. And so, if you find a company that we have listed within these pages is not currently functioning, then an internet search for an alternative should yield results.

AFT — towards the stern.
HW/LW — high water/low water.
NEAPS/SPRINGS — the smallest/biggest tides in the cycle.
RIB (OR RHIB) — rigid hull inflatable boat.
SLACK WATER — for any given place, the point in the tide where there is no current.
SMB/DSMB — surface marker buoy/delayed surface marker buoy.
SS/MV — steamship/motor vessel.

Introduction

"What do you see down there?" is the question that I am most frequently asked when discussion turns to my penchant for underwater exploration about the UK's coastline. For me and everyone that frequently ventures below the surface here, the answer will begin with musings of a nutrient-rich ecosystem, colourful jewel-anemone-splattered reef walls, opportunities to explore shallow sites from the shore, wartime wrecks, diver-enveloping shoals of fish, giant barrel jellies, lobsters and large, fast agile animals like sharks and seals, to reel off just a few.

Smaller creatures draw our attention too. Firework anemones in tubes, common prawns standing "shoulder" to "shoulder" in cracks and miniature molluscs and nudibranchs that resemble something usually found within a packet of jelly sweets crawl about the reef.

Moreover, it is not only the variety of temperate sea creatures that lures the diver into this environment. Simply the geological make-up of an area is a reason to explore. Sea caves, groups of rocks breaking up an otherwise sandy seabed or a set of submerged pinnacles found further from land, barely breaking the surface all create an otherworldly yet alluring atmosphere.

The remnants of our maritime, wartime and naval history attract adventurers with a "lust for rust" underwater too. Many examples of these wrecked and sunken vessels of yesteryear remain relatively intact or at least do their best to appear reasonably identifiable as being ship or even submarine-shaped. Their former working parts now a habitat, breeding and feeding ground for the critters and flora ensconced there. This in turn provides an adventure playground and museum for visiting divers. In this book we visit impressive wrecks such as the torpedoed World War II US Liberty ship *James Eagan Layne* and Dorset's M-class *M2* submarine which sank in tragic circumstances in the 1930s. We head north to the Orkney Islands, exploring several examples of some of the deadliest ships ever built, the World War I German fleet scuttled at Scapa Flow.

Around the UK, the cool water is tinged with a blue-green hue of various gradients, thanks due to its plankton-rich content and this is the foundation for life here. When exactly we choose to enter the sea depends on several factors. Conditions for the diver vary from dark and challenging, through to clear and bright with ample natural light, even at depth. The state of the tide can make or break a dive too. *Neap tides*, the lowest of the high tides, often bring with them better visibility thanks due to minimal water movement. *Spring tides*, the highest of the high tides, are avoided by some divers owing to the possibility of poor visibility brought by large volumes of moving water plus stronger currents and shorter slack windows. However, springs can be a good time to dive deeper sites as low water will be the lowest it can possibly be. The annual algal bloom around May can keep the underwater explorer out of the water for a few weeks as visibility can be reduced to not much more than that of a vegetable soup. Shipwreck sites are dived during a period of *slack water*, the point at which the tide begins to turn and where there is no water moving either way. A cove or bay sat in the lee of the wind or with nil to light wind present or for the preceding days can produce the best conditions for that kind of destination, with the sea state most likely to be calm and the water clear. Sea lochs afford the diver more protection from inclement weather combined with easy water access, especially with heavy camera equipment in hand. A patch of fair weather leading up to a dive trip can yield great results underwater as well but windy conditions above a force four are avoided at sea.

The generally accepted diving *season* in the UK begins around Easter, when the cycle of marine life slowly begins to rotate once again. This continues through to late September or October when sea surface and shallow water temperatures can reach 20°C in the south. Certain months are more favourable for spotting different species underwater too. The grey triggerfish usually begins to appear along the south coast at specific spots, usually wrecks, once August has arrived. The grey triggerfish is an example of a species more commonly found in warmer water across the Atlantic for the rest of the year. Blue sharks begin to arrive in May and June. To find these epipelagic animals requires a longer journey out to sea, along with a little patience. Yet, when trying to locate any kind of wildlife in the sea, having knowledge of its behaviour can improve the success rate.

Winter in the temperate seas brings with it the challenges of diving in cold water — below double figures — and dressing properly for the part becomes a greater consideration. Yet, for some, an official season doesn't exist at all and to simply be within this underwater world whatever the conditions is gratifying enough.

Our exploration of the sea and oceans, temperate or not, occasionally reveals evidence of human interference detrimental to the marine environment. Examples come in the form of sections of barren seabed once home to the slow-growing pink sea fan, raked clean of life by scallop trawling. We see wrecks and reefs draped with discarded or lost commercial fishing gear, plus of course we make discoveries of plastic waste anywhere in the water from the surface to the seabed. Thankfully, our impact on these wild places is slowly being recognised with organisations such as Natural England, and charities like the Blue Marine Foundation and the Marine Conservation Society campaigning for the protection, conservation and restoration of the ocean's health. These important groups also monitor and address a wide spread of issues surrounding commercial over-fishing practices. We as individuals,

DIVING THE KYARRA STUART PHILPOTT

whether underwater explorers or not, can make a difference by choosing carefully what and how we consume. As divers, I believe that we all have a duty to take on the role of "citizen environmentalists", raising public awareness of the struggle that the seas and oceans face at our hands. Perhaps this book will go some way to help increase awareness of what there is to preserve.

The experiences behind the words and images within this book have been delivered to you by some of the greatest champions of our temperate seas from around the UK. Our collective time spent underwater documenting these findings amounts to thousands of hours. I am thrilled to be able to bring together our photographic work, diving experience and voices in the form of this collaborative publication. Many of the dive sites featured within these pages already appear regularly in avid UK divers' log books. Others are visited by only those with local knowledge and some rarely see divers at all. All are special in some way to those who have contributed, evidence for those to whom the UK underwater is still a mystery that once you tame these wild and temperate seas there really are some magnificent experiences to be had.

It is a privilege to be able to raise awareness of the marine flora and fauna that live within this environment too, because globally, our planet beneath the waves whether temperate, tropical or polar, remains for the many, out of sight and out of mind.

Will Appleyard
July 2020

DORSET
by Will Appleyard

Three quarters of the length of Dorset's coastline are grandly labelled the "Jurassic Coast". This UNESCO World Heritage Site spans roughly 95 miles and charts 185 million years of Earth's intriguing geological history. Some of the United Kingdom's most notable landforms stand here including Lulworth Cove, Old Harry Rocks, the Isle of Portland, Chesil Beach and Durdle Door. For the diver, the intrigue continues below the waterline too with a colossal collection of doomed naval history strewn over the seabed, reefs and rock formations.

Swanage, Portland and Weymouth are the main hubs for boats and dive centres, servicing the most popular sites in Dorset. At the weekends, boats are full of familiar faces, be it clubs or locals who repeatedly dive their favourite wrecks and reefs here.

CHESIL COVE AT ITS BEST

The ride out to these dive sites is reason alone to go out to sea, absorbing some of the south coast's most spectacular scenic views while preparing your equipment en route.

The range of diving varies from introductory accessible wrecks in 15m or less of water, to drift dives (especially along the eastern side of Portland, where it is possible to find cannon balls) and then deeper wrecks that still deliver interesting finds for the investigative diver. Although perhaps with fewer options than Devon and Cornwall, the shore diving here is fairly reliable in terms of creatures, features and good visibility, wind direction depending. The seabed is reasonably flat too in comparison to those aforementioned counties, yet the sites popular with divers during the summer months still throng with life.

SWANAGE PIER
50°36'29.5"N 1°57'03.5"W

TOMPOT BLENNY   DAMIAN BROWN

Why dive Swanage Pier? Well, to quote vintage mountaineer George Mallory "because it's there". Although this site is anything but Everest. Swanage Pier can be considered several things: an introductory UK dive, a filler between or after more challenging local boat dives, a testing ground for new equipment or merely somewhere for a jolly good bimble, with or without a camera.

The usual entry point for divers is from the concrete steps by the public toilets on the left-hand side as you walk towards the sea. This is a prime parking spot too, although there are trolleys available to use by the pier entrance if you don't get there early enough.

The pontoon behind Divers Down is for their boat access only, although the diver in this image appears to have sought permission to bend those rules. There is a small entry fee to be paid by divers and "strollers" and this helps fund the pier's expensive upkeep.

Just because it is shallow, Swanage Pier should not be sniffed (or scoffed or sneered) at as a dive site. Several accomplished underwater photographers have taken award-winning photographs under this largely wooden structure. Its 4–5m depth range means that natural light is usually excellent and for the photographer or voyeur, obliging subjects are plentiful. The tompot blenny, an ambassador for UK diving, is a common creature found here. This blenny is a bottom-dwelling fish with a big head, large red and blue eyes and an inquisitive nature. It is the largest of the British blennies, an orange-brown colour with two tentacles on its head. The male has the job of guarding the eggs once a female has laid them and he also takes on the jobs of fertilisation and general housekeeping.

Other resident marine life includes several species of wrasse, like for instance the ballan wrasse, a striking yellow-brown fish. Look for snakelocks anemones, with their green and purple tentacles, often sat on rocks or debris. Crabs — mostly velvet swimmers and edibles. From time to time bass scoot past, hunting. The lumpsucker makes an appearance in spring, during breeding time. Found in deeper water for the balance of the year, these ball-shaped big-lipped fishes have suckers that enable them to stick to rocks. The male, which has an orange-red belly during the breeding season, guards the eggs for a month before they hatch, keeping them oxygenated with wafts of his tail.

Although the pier can be dived at any time, more can be made of the limited depth at high tide. Be careful when you reach the far end, as this area is popular with anglers. Boats come alongside on the town/bay side (or on the left as heading out to sea) and this can stir up the viz. A buoyed swimming area means that the dive centre's boats give the right/eastern side a wider birth. Regardless, always be mindful of boat traffic anywhere around (rather than under) the pier. Propellers are not your friend!

Move away to the east into the seagrass and you will be in pipefish territory. They are well-camouflaged, with brown markings and look more like a snake with a long face and beak than a fish. The seabed here changes from rock to sand.

Adjacent to the Victorian pier are the remains of the old pier. This area is directly accessible from Divers Down's pontoon, behind the shop (seek permission from the shop to use this first). It is a brighter dive, as none of its decking remains. Losing your bearings is easy here owing to the curved shape of the pier's remaining posts and lack of any overhead structure to guide you.

Swanage Pier is by no means challenging, nor is it epic. Yet, there are few places in the UK where divers can park right by the sea, next to both a café and a dive centre. Onlookers cast a quizzical look over the divers about the pier. I still haven't worked out whether they consider us the brave explorers that we believe we are, or whether they just think that we're weird.

PIER REAR ENTRY   ANA RANCAÑO

CORKWING WRASSE KIRSTY ANDREWS

- There is little current at any state of the tide but entry and exit is easier at higher water, especially on springs.

- Head for Swanage town centre where the pier is well signposted and can't be missed. Get there early for the pick of the best parking.

4–5m

SS KYARRA
50°34'54.0"N 1°56'39.0"W

BOLLARDS USED FOR TYING THE SHIP OFF — STUART PHILPOTT

The *Kyarra* was a Scottish-built steamship produced for the Australasian United Steam Navigation Company. This is one of the most famous shipwrecks along the Dorset coast and local dive centres never seem to have trouble filling a boat when advertising a trip here. The dive site suits advanced level divers and above and in good visibility is an adventurous dive. Owned by Kingston BSAC, she is 126m long, a beast of a dive site and spacious enough to accommodate several boat loads of divers at any one time.

The *Kyarra*, en route to Sydney, Australia, prior to her demise, was packed full of "general cargo" along with hundreds of Australian soldiers. The vessel was sent to the bottom by *UB-57* on 26 May 1918 just off Anvil Point, Isle of Purbeck.

For ease of navigation, simply follow the debris or remember that her stern faces west with the bow facing east. Skippers like to drop their divers amidships where one of the four boilers can be clearly seen just away from the main wreckage, with the other three remaining inside. The seabed appears at 32m and the highest piece of metal is at 23m amidships (tide depending) and so a great place to take a final look around when your bottom time becomes too lean. The *Kyarra* is a decent nitrox or short-ish air dive.

There are plenty of penetrable areas along the length of these remains, however extra care should be taken during low visibility. The wreck still shows off many recognizable pieces of hardware including winching equipment, engine, propeller shaft, railings, chains, bollards, rudder and the steering mechanism at the stern.

The *Kyrra* has given up some interesting finds over the years, although having been dived continuously since its discovery in the 1960s, much of the really interesting stuff has already been pilfered. However, she is not totally threadbare and it is said that her holds do still contain more of her loot in the form of perfume, wine and champagne bottles, porcelain teeth, fabrics and gold, silver and brass watches, ornate tiles and medical supplies. Today, divers are encouraged not to take souvenirs from these watery time capsules, however Divers Down shop and dive centre on Swanage Pier have a display cabinet full of some of the aforementioned artefacts recovered in earlier times.

FINDS IN DIVERS DOWN

Slack water is essential: -1hr and +6hr HW Dover. After a period of good weather the visibility should be on your side, but it is usually better at the HW slack.

A very short boat ride away from Swanage Pier with charter operators. RIBs can be launched at Kimmeridge.

ROPES OFF AT SWANAGE

23–32m

MV AEOLIAN SKY
50°30'34.4"N 2°08'24.8"W

INSPECTING THE INTERIOR IN GOOD VIZ — JASON BROWN

This Greek freighter built in 1978 is a monster of a wreck at 148m long. The *Aeolian Sky* was carrying general cargo when she sank in 1979 under tow during bad weather, a day after colliding with the German vessel *Anna Knuppel*. The crew was helicoptered to safety. After the sinking, salvage divers recovered many items including the propeller and it is rumoured (according to Dave down the pub) that of the million Seychelles rupee bank notes stored in her sickbay, many still remain missing today. Her size and spread of cargo, which ranges from Land Rovers and trucks to tractors and glass bottles makes the *Sky* a multi-dive site. She now lies on her port side standing proud of the seabed, resembling the kind of wreck that one might find stoved into the side of a northern Red Sea reef, just a little greener perhaps. The shallowest parts (the starboard side hull) are at 18–20m and the seabed at 30m, plus or minus the odd metre, tide depending.

The stern points roughly north. The huge rudder lolls to one side. One of the most obvious features to discover on the opposite (deck) side in front of the stern winch is the funnel. It has broken free and is angled toward the seabed. The bridge then sits in front with the railings and the companionways easily identifiable. Move further towards the bow from the funnel and every couple of metres thereafter each of seven or eight 60cm diameter masts lie on their sides.

One of the masts is more prominent than the rest at 3m in diameter, around amidships and this one has a pulley on top and a winch either side at deck level. The holds are vast and it is possible to drop into them to join the shoals of bib (pouting) and pollack hiding there. Various sections of the *Sky* are penetrable including the engine room, however caution should be taken when attempting to do this and if the visibility is anything but excellent, then really don't take the risk.

The wreck was cleared from the surface by explosives shortly after sinking, which has produced a tangled mess of metal and plenty of easy over hangs to explore. The exposed part of the hull (the west side) is now covered with marine flora and fauna, which includes the dazzling jewel anemone, beaming bright pinks and yellows under torch light. The hull almost resembles a sloping seabed at first glance, which can be quite disorientating until one pops back over the top to the more interesting deck level (eastern side).

Moving forward further still, the anchor winch sits on the bow at 20m and the starboard anchor is still in place, lying against the hull. To the east of this, a pair of Land Rover chassis have been spewed onto the seabed. Visibility can be exceptional after a spell of good weather, reaching up to 15m. When it is that good expect a super dive and if possible use nitrox to maximize bottom time. Failing that, explore it for a second or third time with a cylinder of good old-fashioned 21% breathing air.

Visibility is often better at high water slack: -2hrs and +3hrs HW Portland. Don't forget your torch and take an SMB for the ascent.

Swanage, Portland and Weymouth dive centres for boats and fills.

18–30m

DIVERS FIN OVER ONE OF SEVERAL HUGE MASTS   JASON BROWN

HMS M2
50°34'36.7"N 2°33'59.0"W

HMS M2   RAF MUSEUM LONDON

HMS *M2* is an intact 296ft M-Class submarine which sits upright on the seabed in 35m of water. This experimental vessel tragically sank in January 1932 with the loss of all 60 of her crew. Originally, she was equipped with a small Parnall Peto sea-going biplane with folding wings which was stowed in a hanger on the pressure hull (deck) when not in use. It was lifted on and off the vessel by a small crane, seen here in the black and white image. It is believed that either a fault with the hanger door or it being left open led to her demise, but the truth went down with her to the seabed.

The wreck is found a couple of miles off shore towards the eastern end of Chesil Beach in Lyme Bay. Local dive boats launch from the marina on the eastern side of Portland, so the journey can take 50 minutes around Portland Bill and through a treacherous section of sea at its tip known as "the race". The journey on a day of fair weather is half of the fun. Passing the prison on the east side, following the cliffs and eventually rounding the bill the boat passes a stack of rock called Pulpit Rock and then peels away from the isle for the more open water where the wreck now sits.

Once descending the shotline, this impressive submarine appears from the gloom when approaching a depth of 20m (if landing right on the conning tower, the shallowest part, that is). At 28m the pressure hull begins and if diving on air, this is a great place to call your maximum depth. Drop over the side and descend to the seabed and you will find yourself at 32–33m — nitrox territory.

Navigating the *M2* is easy, regardless of the available light, with your only options being stern to bow and back, or vice versa, depending on where the shotline has put you. The tall conning tower (the personnel hatch and crew's viewing point) and hanger are clearly identifiable in the centre of the submarine, with the hanger now a habitat for big cod and

ON THE CONNING TOWER — STUART PHILPOTT

pouting. The hanger is the only penetrable part of this wreck but it is tight and very silty. The interior of the main wreck is out of bounds — it still contains the remains of her crew and is classed as a protected wreck.

Conger eels live here, sometimes just a head in view and others just the tail. Many of them are enormous. Crabs and lobster live anywhere that they can find some shelter and starfish are scattered about the seabed. Brightly coloured sponges and dead man's fingers are present in patches all over the structure's surface. Jewel anemones decorate each side of the conning tower, attractive when lit by a torch and you will see more tompot blennies in holes on this wreck than on any other.

The visibility can vary from a challenging 2–3m in the dark, to a glorious 10m plus with the wreck laid out for you in all her glory. To dive her requires a day of fine weather, which you will be thankful for during your boat rides to and from the site. Some previous UK diving experience will enhance your enjoyment of the *M2*. Like waiting for a weather window on Everest, once it's diveable, you most probably won't be the only divers on her. The *M2* is a spectacular wreck and is probably the finest example of a submarine to dive on anywhere in the UK.

- Slack water is -4hrs HW (neaps only) and +3hrs HW, Portland.

- Portland, Weymouth, West Bay and Lyme Regis operators run shuttles.

20–33m

CHESIL COVE
50°33'32.4"N 2°26'54.1"W

CUTTLEFISH

COMMON LOBSTER   ALEX GIBSON

Chesil Beach is a place of contrasts, a wolf in sheep's clothing if you like. It takes the brunt of the gnarliest of weather funnelling up the widest part of the English Channel from the south-west, producing some seriously violent wave action when the weather is rough. And yet, when the wind direction is either easterly or better still non-existent, the cove couldn't be more inviting to anyone who enjoys being in or on the water, as it sits at the eastern end of this 18-mile long beach, nestled into Portland at its southern tip. During a weekend of fine conditions, finding a parking space anywhere near the top of the ramp with the best beach access for divers (to the left of the Cove House Inn pub) can be tricky if you don't get there early. The alternative is to drive as near to the elevated sea wall as possible, dump your gear off and park somewhere further down the road.

The beach drops steeply on entry and then gradually deeper thereafter, eventually levelling off at around 12–18m. The most scenic areas to dive are between the disused sewer pipeline, which starts more or less in front of Quiddles Café (south of the ramp) and the area which falls across the Cove House Inn (great food and beer). Here, depths range from 6–18m and the large pebbles eventually decrease in size giving way to vast sand patches. Overall, the most interesting scenery is to be found in the 8–14m range amongst the rocks, pebbles and assorted unidentifiable metal wreckage (of the *Preveza*), now a habitat for an abundance of sea life in late spring and summer.

Chesil Cove has numerous underwater "trails" but can easily be dived straight in-and-out like any other beach. It is easy to get disorientated when submerged, but the rule of thumb in the cove navigation-wise is: out is west and home is east.

The striking John dory lives here and during the spring it is easy to find them feeding on shoals of juvenile fish species among the bigger rocks and the tall weed. Angler fish (monkfish) hunt here too, although being a bottom-dwelling, motionless species for the most part, it is harder to spot. Chesil Cove sees a reasonable amount of spearfishing too, so any reports of a creature like this in the area will often travel quickly in that community.

Plenty of cat sharks (aka dogfish) lie about the sand. They are lazy looking creatures, with big dark eyes and fabulous brown spotty markings, never moving more than a few metres at a time. Siding right up to one on the seabed is no problem at all. Purple-tipped snakelocks anemone are commonplace and animals such as Leach's spider crab and the tiny snakelocks shrimp live in a symbiotic relationship with them, using the anemone's venomous tentacles for their own protection. Squid eggs flap about below over-hanging rocks in the deeper sections like blonde dreadlocks. It is almost always possible to find lobster during a cove dive, plus bundles of edible and spider crabs — they are two a penny. Curious cuttlefish live here also. If you are diving with a camera with a large dome port, point the lens in the creature's direction and it may move in closer to inspect its own reflection, lining itself up for a great shot in the process. And don't forget to look up because on a good day the surface is often always visible from the seabed. For the photographer, the cove can be a place to operate bathed in exceptional natural light.

There are several ways to exit the water here post-dive: remove your fins and walk out like a pro; beach yourself fully kitted and deal with removing your kit while rolling around the beach before trying to get up; or, have someone on the shore to help you by carrying your weights and camera up the beach for you. All of those methods are perfectly acceptable and all are attempted during a busy shore diving day. Leaving the water when waves are breaking on the beach is to say the least, problematic. Towing a surface marker buoy is sensible owing to the likely presence of some small fishing or pleasure craft.

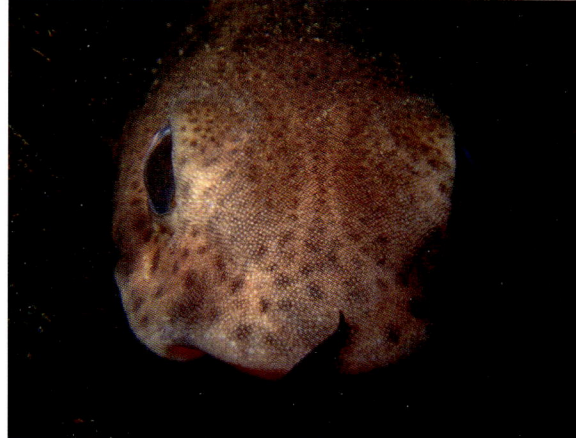

CATSHARK — LLOYD JONES

SPIDER CRAB — ROB ROSLYN

- Dive only when sea conditions are benign. Easier exits at HW but any time, day or night is diveable.

- Head for Portland on the A354 Portland Beach Road, drive up Chiswell and unload gear at the top of Brandy Row, where the ramp to the beach begins.

0–18m

FACT FILE

GETTING THERE Dorset dive sites are well served by dive charters from Swanage, Weymouth and Portland. RIBs can be launched at Kimmeridge and Castletown.

ANYTHING ELSE? There are many more sites to choose from, especially wrecks. For those suitably qualified and equipped, the P&O liner *Salsette* (50m to the seabed) is a perennial favourite.

DIVE OPERATIONS Kit hire and air fills from:
Divers Down, Swanage — www.diversdownswanage.co.uk (also boat charters)
Swanage Boat Charters, Swanage — www.kyarra.com (boat charter only)
Underwater Explorers, Portland — www.underwaterexplorers.co.uk
Dive Beyond, Portland — www.divebeyond.co.uk (also boat charters)
O'Three, Portland — www.othree.co.uk (equipment only)
Skin Deep, Portland — www.skindeepdiving.co.uk (boat charter)
Scimitar Diving, Portland — www.scimitardiving.co.uk (also boat charters)
Old Harbour Dive Centre, Weymouth — oldharbourdivecentre.co.uk (also charters)
West Bay Charters, West Bay — www.westbaycharters.co.uk (boat charter).

A DIVE CATAMARAN ON A FLAT CALM SEA

M2 BOW AND TORPEDO TUBES
STUART PHILPOTT

TORBAY

by Dan Bolt

Comprising the towns of Torquay, Paignton and Brixham, Torbay is a four mile wide sheltered bay in south Devon. In 2007 it was designated as a UNESCO Geopark, recognising its landscape as being of international geological significance. It is now known as the English Riviera Geopark. The many different geological features found in the bay shape 20 beaches and coves, as well as a 20-mile stretch of the South West Coast Path.

All this geology doesn't stop at the low water mark however. These features mean that just a short distance from shore a diver can be swimming over lush meadows of eelgrass, through sunken caves, over rich reef systems and amongst countless juvenile fish in large nurseries.

There are areas of low, medium and high water-flow, each providing a habitat to

HOPE'S NOSE, TORBAY

specialist groups of species. There are plenty of nationally rare creatures that are actually quite common here, and being on the southern edge of the UK it gets quite a few warm-water species found in only a few other spots in England.

The beaches vary from rock and pebbles through heavy and into fine sand. There are towering cliffs and secluded coves too. Sadly, the main body of the seabed in the bay is a silt/mud mix; meaning that any heavy easterly wind will stir up the sediment and reduce the visibility to zero for a few days. That isn't all bad news though. Because of the occasionally lower visibility, the kelp-line in Torbay tends to stop at around 6m and some species of anemone and sponge can be found much shallower than in many clearer parts of the West Country.

BABBACOMBE
50°28'45.0"N 3°30'33.9"W

JOHN DORY BEING CLEANED

ANEMONE SHRIMP

1–10m

One of the most popular spots in Torbay for shore diving, Babbacombe is easy to love due to straightforward water access and the variety of marine life throughout the year. It is perhaps best known as one of the finest places in the UK to see large numbers of cuttlefish. In the late spring and early summer they come into the shallow bay to find a mate and lay their eggs amongst the tall weeds, where the relatively warm water speeds up the growth of their offspring. This isn't a straightforward process as keeping a mate from other rivals often involves violent clashes between males, and even desperate females looking to force out a successfully-paired competitor.

Around six weeks after laying, tiny juvenile cuttlefish start to hatch and immediately turn into perfectly-formed hunting machines. Despite being just a few centimetres long these babies have all their parents' abilities to colour and shape shift, ambush prey and squirt a mini-cloud of ink if threatened.

Despite a commercial fishery covering all of Torbay, it is not unusual to see large numbers of cuttles here. Swimming due north off the slipway will take you to one of the preferred breeding grounds, but as the egg-laying season draws on they can be found all over the bay, wherever there is suitably available weed.

In the summer and autumn there is a good chance to see warm water visitors such as Montague's blennies and anemone shrimps. Both can be found below the boardwalk to the west. The blennies are best looked for at high tide on the shallow rock faces, whereas the shrimp can be found in the large numbers of snakelocks anemones about 25m due north of that

CUTTLEFISH FIGHTING

point. There are often sightings of octopus in spring and summer, and in autumn John dory come into the shallows after dark to be cleaned by Leach's spider crabs. This is possibly the only place in the UK where this behaviour has been recorded.

Chat to any local diver and they are likely to reference most points of interest from "Mushroom Rock". This aptly named feature lies 30 degrees and around 100m from the slipway, and is actually the middle of three large rocks (around 4m tall) that stand proud of the sandy, rocky seabed. It has a large overhang that has many dead man's fingers, and the most accessible colony of jewel anemones for miles around.

Heading north of Mushroom Rock you'll reach a large area of sand, home to burrowing anemones, sand-mason worms and, in summer, painted gobies making their nests under discarded scallop shells.

There is one final reason to dive at Babbacome, and that's to do a night-dive. Three year-round residents are species that glow under blue light: the snakelocks, jewel and burrowing anemones all display this behaviour. This is an utterly unique experience. After dark you'll also very often encounter juvenile squid out hunting over the sand, some will even turn your torch-light to their advantage and attack the tiny critters attracted to it.

- No currents to worry about here, but there are lots of slippery rocks to walk over on a low spring tide. Be wary of boat-traffic, as well as anglers plus old hooks and line if you dive from the steps at the end of the pier.

- Beach Road, Torquay, TQ1 3LU. Drive carefully down the very steep, winding road to the car park.

BEACON COVE
50°27'26.6"N 3°31'25.0"W

Torbay has an estimate 80 hectares of protected seagrass beds. Those in danger of boat or anchor damage are marked with distinctive buoys. The beds at Beacon Cove and around the Millstones are about twelve football pitches in size.

Looking out from the beach to the right you'll see the two rocks known as the Millstones. They stand a few metres proud of a large rocky reef that runs out to the south-east of the outer stone and is only 10m deep at most. On it there are dozens of large white *Phallusua mammillata*, the UK's largest sea squirts at about 15cm tall. The outer Millstone has large elephant's hide sponge on its inner edge, and many dead man's fingers on the outer edge.

As nice as the reef is, the main draw of this dive is the seagrass beds made from the plant (not seaweed) *Zostera marina*. If you swim to the Millstones reef along the sandy seabed you will encounter a few small clumps of the plant, but the major part of the bed starts around 50m to the south-east of the beach in around 6–7m of water.

The easiest way to find the best area of seagrass is to follow the bolder field at the base of the cliff (on your left as you look out to sea) for around 6–7 minutes. You'll see plenty of snakelocks anemones and velvet swimming crabs along your way. After a while you should then head south over the sand and very soon, you'll come across dense areas of grass.

This unique habitat is a valuable home to many invertebrate species, and in spring acts as shelter for numerous juvenile fish

MALE AND FEMALE ISOPODS

JUVENILE SNAKELOCKS ANEMONE

as well as a mating ground for cuttlefish. Don't ignore the sand in and around the seagrass, it's home to the sand burrowing brittlestar, eyelash worms and a regular hunting ground for plaice and dab.

🕒 There are no currents to worry about here so you can dive at any state of the tide, although if there is any swell it will be more comfortable at high water.

📍 To get to the beach for this dive it is about a 150m walk around a winding concrete path from Torquay Harbour, Beacon Quay, Torquay, TQ1 2BG.

4–10m

SEA SQUIRTS ON AN ABANDONED POT

LONG-SPINED SEA SCORPION

FLAT ROCK
50°27'43.3"N 3°28'41.1"W

SO MUCH COLOUR TO BE FOUND UNDER THE BOULDERS

Also referred to as the Lead Stone on Admiralty charts, Flat Rock is a low-lying lump of limestone just 200m off Hope's Nose, the northerly headland of Torbay. At less than 100m long and 30m wide, this isn't a huge rock, but it is big enough to be an important nesting site for many seabirds. Please don't be tempted to land here during breeding season as you may get dive-bombed by defensive parents.

Despite its proximity to the shore, as a kayak dive you'll have to paddle the 1.5 miles from the nearest launching site at Meadfoot Beach. It's an interesting stretch of coastline though, and the route takes you past the 40m high Thatcher Rock, another important nesting site. As you round Hope's Nose itself, keep an eye out for grey seals which are often seen around the headland.

The area of interest on this site is the reef which runs out from the north-east edge of the rock. The dive starts below the sheer rock wall on which, because it is north-facing, the kelp only goes down the first few metres and very quickly gives way to elegant anemones, dead man's fingers and daisy anemones. At the base of the wall, a boulder field provides shelter to juvenile bib, and there are lots of hiding places for all five of the UK wrasse species. The larger boulders are topped with plumose anemones, sandalled anemones, and in the shelter of overhangs live patches of jewel anemones in every colour.

Moving north-east from the boulders the seabed rises and falls in a series of gentle ridges as the bedrock breaks through the sand. The heavy sand is perfect anemone habitat and there are dahlia and elegant species in abundance. The rocky ridges have rows of bright white dead man's fingers and plenty of large boring sponges to add a splash of yellow to the reef. Large spider crabs can always be seen here. Edible crabs and lobsters can be found at the base of each ridge, sharing their homes with gravel sea cucumbers and smaller velvet swimming crabs.

Because of the high tidal flows here, you're always in with a chance of seeing a few jellyfish floating by, including the enormous barrels that are often found in large numbers around this coastline.

◐ Should only be dived at slack: -2 or +4 hours HW Torquay. The longer slack is on the flood tide as the rock provides a lee from the tidal current. Avoid on big spring tides.

◉ Kayaks launch from Meadfoot beach; RIBs from Torquay Harbour.

8–15m

FLAT ROCK OFF HOPE'S NOSE

A LARGE BARREL JELLYFISH

DIVING OVER THE COLOURFUL REEF

LONDON BRIDGE
50°27'15.0"N 3°31'07.9"W

LONDON BRIDGE

MARINE LIFE AT THE FOOT OF THE ARCH

3–11m

London Bridge (also known as London Arch) is a natural rock arch formed from Devonian limestone. It is right next to the abandoned Dyer's Quarry.

I like to get here by kayak, launching at either Meadfoot Beach for free, or for a small fee from Torquay Harbour. Both leave you with a little over a half mile paddle along some of Torbay's high limestone cliffs.

From the surface it looks like the arch is the main attraction, but below water there is a large swim-through and the remains of a long-ago spilled cargo, known locally as "The Pipes".

Immediately below the inshore edge of the arch, running south-west to northeast, there is a large crack that opens into a cave and swim-through. From the surface down to around 5m, the walls of the cave are littered with jewel anemones, boring sponge, encrusting sponges and squirts.

CAVE WALLS COVERED IN SPONGES AND ANEMONES

Exit the cave and a few fin strokes to the south-west you'll find the inside edge of the foot of the arch. Because it is north-facing, there is no weed along the rock face and so there are dozens of dead man's fingers and encrusting sponges. Topknot flatfish can be found on the verticals, and tompot blennies are a regular sight too.

Exploring the outer edge of the foot of the arch is easy. If you go clockwise you'll keep the rock on your right shoulder (anti-clockwise, left shoulder). Once back on the south side of the rock you'll be into the kelp again, but it disappears at about 6m. You'll pass a few open cracks with more jewel anemones and eventually at around 11m come across some large metal pipes, some over 6m long. The pipes are spread over quite a large area, and many are home to conger eel, lobster and juvenile fish.

Complete this circular tour by following the rock edge back under the arch. You could actually swim the whole thing in around ten minutes, but with so much to look at and being so shallow it's easy to stay under for more than an hour.

- There are no currents to worry about here but take care if there is any swell running into the cave.

- Kayak launch from Meadfoot beach. RIBs from Torquay Harbour.

MEADFOOT
50°27'26.7"N 3°30'31.0"W

DEAD MAN'S FINGERS

KITTING UP ON THE BEACH

At low tide Meadfoot Beach is over 600m long and a mix of sand, pebbles, boulders and rock pools. At high tide the accessible portions reduce significantly and at the top of a spring tide, very little of the beach remains at all. At the western end (near the café and toilets) there is a pedestrian-only slipway onto the beach which is also the best spot for diving this area.

Navigating the dive is easy — just head straight out, roughly south-east. If you're fit enough you can aim for Shag Rock (also known as East Shag Rock), but it's 350m from shore so only tackle this if you are certain of your abilities.

In the shallows just off the beach the seabed is heavy sand lying between outcrops of kelp-covered bedrock. The sand attracts a good number of flatfish, while in the summer months bootlace weed provides shelter for hundreds of juvenile fish and packs of bass on the hunt.

Heading further out, the sand turns to pebbles and the rocks get taller. Many of the larger outcrops have tall north-facing edges and little in the way of weed growth. These weed-free areas are a great place to look for nudibranchs and the ever inquisitive tompot blenny. Beyond the rocks there is a large area of heavy sand which would normally be the place to turn around. But it may be worth spending a few moments there as it's a favourite spot for red mullet. If you venture too far out on the sand and feel a current you should pay attention to it and turn back to the beach.

If heading for Shag Rock, you'll have to swim over this sand for five or six minutes and will eventually re-join a larger reef system in about 10m of water. The rock itself has a steep northern edge (facing the beach) with dozens of anemones and

MATING NUDIBRANCHS

encrusting sponges. The unusually shallow colonies of sandalled and jewel anemones can find themselves out of the water for a short while on a low spring tide. On the south-western corner, large gullies standing 4m tall sink into the heavy sand and form a rich reef with hundreds of plumose anemones, many species of sponges, dahlia anemones and dozens of blennies, nudibranchs and crabs.

🕒 Diving from the beach is best done around high tide. You only need to worry about currents if swimming out to Shag Rock, which should only be done on slack: -2 or +4 hours HW Torquay.

RED MULLET

📍 Meadfoot Sea Rd, Torquay, TQ1 2LQ.

2–12m

SHOALSTONE
50°24.105'N 3°29.831' W

Diving at Shoalstone is all about timing. Unlike all the other shore dives in Torbay, this one you need to do at slack water.

Entering the water either directly below the steps from the car park, or over the rocks to the eastern end of the walkway, this is an easy dive to navigate. Head straight out (roughly north) and the kelp quickly gives way to weed-covered bedrock and sandy patches. Pretty soon bright yellow boring sponges will start to appear with lots of other low-lying ascidians and carpets of trumpet anemones.

At any point of this dive you stand a very high chance of seeing nudibranchs. Shoalstone is a hotspot for the nationally rare *Okenia elegans*, and over 30 species of nudibranch have been recorded at this one site alone. In late spring and early summer is not unusual to see dozens of slugs wherever you look, with different species favouring different habitats. Mid-way over the reef you'll start to see large stands of sea beard, a hydroid which looks like tall yellow feathers standing proud of the rock. This is a favourite habitat for many nudibranchs to lay their egg-masses. It is also a hunting ground for the quite scary-looking skeleton shrimp.

Swimming out further still, the ridges in the rock become more pronounced and topped with large, colourful plumose anemones. Once you hit mud at around 15m it's not worth going any further out. Instead you can head back in and take a bearing parallel to the coast to stay on your preferred depth contour.

The outer parts have been home to triggerfish, octopus and lumpsuckers over the years, and there's always the chance of an encounter with one of the friendly local seals as you swim across the reef.

POLYCERA QUADRILINEATA

COLOURFUL PLUMOSE ANEMONES

TORBAY: SHOALSTONE

🕐 Slack water doesn't follow the same pattern here as the other side of Torbay. Instead you need to dive bang-on high or low-water. On neap tides you can jump in at about -1 hour HW Torquay and any currents you encounter will be light and perfectly manageable. On spring tides slack water will not last for long with the current quickly changing direction. It's worth using an SMB here due to the possibility of boat traffic.

📍 Shoalstone car park, Berry Head Rd, Brixham, TQ5 9FT.

4–15m

SHOALSTONE AERIAL VIEW

SKELETON SHRIMP

OKENIA ELEGANS

FACT FILE

GETTING THERE Launching facilities are available at the following locations: Polly Steps, Old Quay Street, Teignmouth (the carpark and slipway are at the end of the port buildings) — www.teignmouthharbour.com/harbour/facilities; RIBs and kayaks can be launched from Torquay Harbour, Beacon Quay, Torquay — www.tor-bay-harbour.co.uk — and kayaks can also be launched from Meadfoot Beach.

ANYTHING ELSE? There are so many sites to choose from. The SS *Bretagne* was a collier which sank after a collision in fog in 1918 and is now an upright wreck in 28m with recognisable features including a spare propeller on the deck. The *Emsstrom*, Torbay's newest wreck, sank while under tow in 2013 and is very accessible with depths ranging from 12–30m.

DIVE OPERATIONS
Teign Diving Centre, Teignmouth — teigndivingcentre.co.uk (air and boat charter)
Nautilus Dive and RIB charter, Brixham Harbour — nautilusdivecharters.com
Dive Torquay, Meadfoot Beach — divetorquay.co.uk

DIVERS ENTERING AT BABBACOMBE

SQUID AT NIGHT

PLYMOUTH
by Will Appleyard

Plymouth, Devon, is a location with centuries of maritime history. It lies between the rivers Plym and Tamar which flow into Plymouth Sound. The city began its steady coastal sprawl in the Middle Ages as a small fishing village. Tudor times saw it grow into a town focused on fishing but also commercial imports like fruit, sugar, hops and wine. Sir Frances Drake was born here. A long list of firsts unfurls from Plymouth, one of these being the construction of the world's first offshore lighthouse. Several versions stood before the current incarnation was built on Eddystone Rocks. At her feet lies one of the south coast's most impressive reefs.

Plymouth has played an important role in supporting the Royal Navy through much conflict over the last six centuries. The city was largely destroyed during World War II,

EDDYSTONE LIGHTHOUSE

having suffered the bombing raids of the Blitz. Today, the naval base at Devonport remains the largest in Europe, home to British war ships, nuclear submarines and NATO vessels.

With ropes off from Plymouth, we are also able to enter blue shark territory and when sea conditions allow, visit the submerged mini mountain of Hatt Rock. Plymouth has both historic and purpose-sunk wrecks, vibrant reefs, submerged pinnacles, gullies and drifts. Perfectly situated at the border between Devon and Cornwall, due to the lay of the land there are dive sites *almost* whatever the weather, with decent back-ups in the Sound. When you can get out to sea the range and quality of diving is hard to beat and some of the highlights are included here.

SS JAMES EAGAN LAYNE
50°19'32.4"N 4°14'39.0"W

A DIVER EXPLORES THE HOLDS

The World War II Liberty Ship SS *James Eagan Layne* is one of the most famous wreck dive sites in the UK. The "JEL" was built by the Delta Ship Building Company, New Orleans, Louisiana, USA in 1944. Today she rests on a sandy seabed in Whitsand Bay, south-east Cornwall, close to the Devon border.

Liberty ships were a class of cargo ship manufactured in the US, designed to be built quickly and reasonably cheaply in order to service the rapid pace of demand of the war effort. This example, named after a merchant seaman killed earlier in the war, was carrying "government stores" or military cargo from Barry in Wales, destined for Ghent, Belgium, following the conclusion of the Battle of the Bulge in the January prior. She was sighted off Eddystone Rocks and badly damaged by a torpedo strike from U-boat *U-399* on 21 March 1945, but not immediately sunk. All of her crew of 69 survived the attack. The 129m-long ship was then towed into Whitsand Bay and beached, where she remained visible with her masts breaking the surface for over 20 years.

Remarkably, for many years divers would visit the wreck as a shore dive. An exhausting sounding exercise owing to the scramble down to the shoreline with one's equipment to begin with, coupled with a long surface swim out and then back again.

Today, the masts are no longer visible at the surface and she is best explored from a boat. The *JEL* sits upright on the seabed in around 23m of water, making it a perfect novice UK wreck exploration but offering plenty of interest for all levels of diver. The prominent bow is a good place to start the dive and the shallowest point, beginning at around 12m below the surface after much of it collapsed to starboard in 2019. Here, before following the usual route down into her holds, the outer part of the bow is worth investigating first. This area is covered with anemones and fish life from the deck to the seabed.

The wreck's interior, which would have originally consisted of five holds in total, is easily accessible and it is possible to swim through the length of her in one dive. The deck level is missing in part and so it is easy to leave the wreck at any time as well as through the hold hatches which are clear of debris. There are gaping holes in parts of the port and starboard sides too — have a look out through these as you can often see decent-sized bass around the wreck. Inside, the holds are cavernous and light pours in from above. This is a habitat for large shoals of bib and pollack.

Towards the now separate stern is the exit point (if starting at the bow). Once outside, a spread of sandy seabed and a debris field leads the diver to the torn-away stern, located on the port side or on the right as you leave the holds.

Alternatively, consider carrying out your dive in reverse, starting by cruising over the top deck from the bow, entering the wreck from the stern and completing your dive at the bow, where a shotline is usually fixed in place. This too is the perfect area for a safety stop before finally surfacing.

EXITING THE WRECK TOWARDS THE STERN

This site can be dived at any state of the tide.

Just 30 minutes from Plymouth by boat. There is usually a buoy fixed on the bow.

12–23m

EDDYSTONE LIGHTHOUSE
50°10'49.1"N 4°16'00.4"W

JEWEL ANEMONES DAMIAN BROWN

🕐 Can be dived at any time during neap tides, although slack water is advised during springs. This falls at +2.5hrs HW/LW Devonport. The east and south pinnacles are always best dived at slack or on an ebb tide.

0–40m

There are many reasons to love diving Eddystone. First there is the history of the various towers which were built over 200 years, destroyed by fierce weather and replaced. This culminated in the 1888 Douglas Tower which still stands today.

Diving wise, Eddystone is considered one of the best reefs in the south-west. Part of the "Start Point to Plymouth Sound and Eddystone Special Area of Conservation" since 2010, a level of protection is now in place, albeit at the time of writing, the buffer zone was only 200m around the reef base. But it is a good start and means that the use of destructive bottom-towed fishing methods, like scallop trawling, is now prohibited here. Moreover, vulnerable species like hydroids, dead man's fingers, sponges and ross have a stronger chance of survival.

This site's distance from shore, proximity to the cool clear water of the Atlantic and the seabed's coarse light-coloured sand mean that visibility and natural light available at depth can be exceptional. When conditions are at their best, expect some 20m of clarity.

There are seven main entry points and the marks for those are detailed here. Exploration of this wild place starts anywhere from where rock meets the surface, and goes all the way down into the more challenging 40m+ zone. Examples include the east pinnacle. This point begins at around 20m and for accuracy, is best descended upon with a shot and line in the water. The south-east pinnacle begins in the 16m region and over kelp. If

MALE CUCKOO WRASSE

you land on kelp and wish to explore the rocks in more detail, then move deeper, where the kelp will thin out. There is a lot of life however, held within these little watery woodlands.

Exquisite examples of the delicate pink sea fan stand about this protected zone. Colossal boulders splashed like a decorator's radio with millions of jewel anemones tumble into the deep. Urchins and starfish pick the rocks in slow motion and dazzling male cuckoo wrasse vainly seek their own attention in the reflection of masks and camera lens ports. Schools of bass and pollack patrol the water column above the reef and off out into the green/blue.

Eddystone reef is one of many areas extensively surveyed, recorded and mapped by Seasearch, a voluntary group with an interest in sea habitats. Their data is made available to partner organisations and the public, raising awareness of the diversity of marine life within our seas.

This special place suits both rookies and dive gods. Dolphins, minky and fin whales cruise by the rocks and so when back on the boat, keep one eye out to sea.

One hour from Mountbatten. Marks for various pinnacle entries:
Outer north
    50°11'34.3"N 4°15'59.8"W
Inner north
    50°11'04.4"N 4°15'56.3"W
Outer east
    50°11'01.4"N 4°15'19.7"W
East
    50°10'54.3"N 4°15'29.8"W
South-east
    50°10'48.4"N 4°15'43.7"W
Inner west
    50°10'50.0"N 4°16'08.0"W
Outer west
    50°10'58.7"N 4°16'22.4"W.

HATT ROCK
50°10'28.2"N 4°29'10.8"W

ON THE EDGE OF HATT ROCK

If Devon and Cornwall appear kind of foot-shaped on the map, Hatt Rock sits somewhere in the middle below the arch, 14 nautical miles from Plymouth. The site is about ten miles south of Looe if travelling from Cornwall.

Hatt Rock is a wild and remote place, a sunken island or mini flat-topped mountain and one of, if not the, most scenic dive in the south-west. Above water there is nothing but sea for miles looking over every side of the dive boat. The site begins 25m below the surface and the walls are steep, well, vertical. The rock would need grading a 7A or above in climbing terms (hard). The seabed appears at 50–60m below, depending on where you are and is easily visible from the top of the drop off. The water clarity can be so good here that it is easy to find yourself deeper than intended. It is also tempting to head deeper than your equipment or experience might allow. In mountaineering terms, this is known as having "summit fever". Don't succumb to "seabed fever" if not properly equipped to be there.

Unlike some of the shallower pinnacles along the south-west coast with their deep

PLYMOUTH: HATT ROCK

OVERHANGS COVERED WITH JEWEL ANEMONES

kelp forest, Hatt Rock prefers the short back and sides look. The sheer walls are the number one attraction here. Almost every available space has been taken up by the colourful jewel anemone, which come a close second, if not joint first. With (usually) epic south-west coast visibility, diving at Hatt Rock feels like close proximity wing suit flying (see YouTube), cruising in slow motion above the earth in some kind of psychedelic alpine dream. The flat sheer walls are occasionally interrupted by deep gashes in the rock or sections overhanging the face. Look for slipper lobsters here, along with the puffed-up cushion starfish. These creatures are seldom seen at dive sites closer to land along this part of the UK coast. To dive this site with air will be nothing but a short tease. Owing to the 25m starting point, at the very least a nitrox mix should be obligatory, especially if you want to have fun and stay longer. The rock needs a shot placing on it and one should launch a marker buoy for the ascent. Most certainly, Hatt Rock requires good sea conditions to dive owing to its remote, exposed, wild and epically adventurous location.

- Slack water is -3–4hrs and +2–3hrs HW Devonport.

- Approximately one hour from Mountbatten.

25–50m

BLUE SHARKS (SNORKEL)
WAY OFFSHORE

A SHARK INVESTIGATES THE HULL

The seas surrounding the UK are home to several visiting shark species, including the globally distributed, highly migratory blue shark. To find these sleek, slender creatures requires some patience, sea legs, bait and a bucket full of fish innards, or "chum".

The fog we had set out in at 6 am lifts and we motor to a patch of water miles offshore. Fishermen have spotted blue sharks here. We kill the engine on arrival. The sea is flat, quiet except for our own boat noises. Occasionally, a container ship slides past on the horizon. I put trust in the skipper that our small vessel is not actually within the shipping lane. Two buoys are set on a rope and cast off the boat with bait positioned at two different depths — one at 5m and the other at 10m. On the surface, the skipper introduces a slick of oily innards to the current, seeping from a net bag dangled over the side. If the sharks pick up the scent, the animals will be attracted to our chum slick from literally miles away.

Once lured in, we then hope to draw them onto the 10m baited buoy and finally the bait set at 5m, before coming to the surface. If they appear and hang around, we will enter the water, but of course nothing is guaranteed when attempting to photograph wildlife.

Approaching two hours since our arrival, surrounded by nothing but sea and sky, the buoys remain undisturbed in the water and there is not a breath of wind. Our sitting positions morph into lying ones and conversation dries up. I begin to consider that we may have to write this one off. Right on the two hour mark, the deep buoy rapidly bobs under and reappears, then, somewhat more tentatively, so does the shallower one. Finally, the indigo hue of a blue shark's slender back and dorsal fin meet the surface, steadily followed by others. We ready ourselves to slip in with them, reasonably gear-free with just our masks, snorkels, fins, weights and wet suits to pull on. No scuba equipment is required here.

A nibble from one of these epipelagic creatures is unlikely, but we still completely cover our skin with neoprene to prevent an investigation of that nature. Five individuals appear beside the boat in all and the skipper advises us to keep our eyes on the creatures at all times while in the water. But in reality they are the ones keeping an eye on us. The

UP CLOSE AND PERSONAL   DAMIAN BROWN

water clarity is good, sun rays dive into the deep like outstretched fingers and I breath heavily through my snorkel. Horizontal on the surface, ready on the camera's shutter trigger, I track a pair of 2m sharks as they swim a figure of eight between one another and then slip away, out of sight. The duo then reappear exactly where I don't expect them to be. Close, inquisitive encounters become physical ones with snouts bumping my camera lens port. Big, oceanic goggle-eyes designed for the deep ocean appear to almost meet mine at my mask.

Our time in the water is always limited when engaging with wildlife, regardless of depth. We witness just a snapshot of this extraordinary animal's life and behaviour. This is their territory and we are but clumsy yet privileged visitors to it.

Blues are the most heavily fished of the shark species with many millions caught annually, often as by-catch. Of course, their fins continue to command a high price within the despicable shark-finning trade, yet their meat is of very little value at all. The species moves seasonally to higher latitudes in search of abundant prey that includes mainly squid, pelagic and shoaling fish. They produce anywhere from four to 135 pups per litter, born in the spring and summer months after a nine to twelve month gestation period.

🕒 Blues begin to appear off the south coast of Devon and Cornwall from mid to late June and can be found until September. When attempting to locate any form of wildlife, it is never a given that they will appear, however the anticipation of finding these mysterious animals is wholly part of the adventure.

📍 Shark trips: Devon — indeep.co.uk
Cornwall — charleshood.com

0–5m

FACT FILE

GETTING THERE Make sure you head to the correct marina to meet your boat — although only a few minutes via the water, Mountbatten is a 20 minute drive from Sutton Harbour on the town side of Plymouth. Just to confuse you there are also two Yacht Haven marinas.

ANYTHING ELSE? There are wrecks galore, more submerged pinnacles, shallow reefs and back-up dives in the Sound. Book with confidence!

DIVE OPERATIONS
In Deep, Mountbatten Watersports Centre — www.indeep.co.uk
Aquanauts, Vauxhall Street — www.aquanauts.co.uk
Sound Diving, Yacht Haven Quay — www.sounddivingplymouth.co.uk
Plymouth Diving Centre, Queen Annes Battery Marina — plymouthdivingcentre.co.uk

SURFACE INTERVAL ON A HARD BOAT

JEL CARGO
ALEX GIBSON

PORTHKERRIS

by Will Appleyard

Thankfully for the diving community, Porthkerris Cove is not a place that random beach-goers are likely to just chance upon. Hidden on the south side of the Lizard Peninsula, this secluded spot only emerges once one has navigated a rabbit warren of skinny Cornish country roads, passed the village of St Keverne and then navigated a second rabbit warren of skinny Cornish country roads. This place would for sure have met the requirements of any determined 18th-century smuggler. Once the high-sided hedges begin to peter out and the tree-lined roads are replaced by fields, a single track begins to wend seawards until it meets the beach and buildings of Porthkerris Divers.

The cove is overlooked and then flanked on both sides by green-topped steep crumbly cliffs. The pebble beach, lapped by the sea, is several shades of grey with a tide line

MANACLES REEF AERIAL CORNWALL

of coastal deposits left at various stages of its highs and lows. Porthkerris Divers is a family-run business and their house overlooks the dive centre's cool, cabin-style shop, air station and café. A Ministry of Defence building, nothing more than functional in its architecture, to be polite, peers out onto the main shore diving area — Drawna Rocks — as it has done for years.

    Although a peaceful setting, it is no secret among divers and not just British ones, keen European underwater explorers love this place just as much. It is hardly surprising considering how well divers are catered for — besides the diving there's camping and B&B accommodation and a cafe. Beach BBQs are not uncommon and are most welcome after a night dive searching for critters in the shallows just off the beach.

DRAWNA ROCKS
50°08'42.6"N 5°02'53.4"W

JEWEL ANEMONES — ALEX GIBSON

Drawna Rocks, or "Dragon Rocks" (from Cornish) is well protected from anything other than a stiff easterly wind. In such conditions one has no chance of entering, or more importantly, exiting the water safely. Otherwise, this quiet cove, miles away from anything vaguely like a main road is simply ideal for shore diving. It is possible to achieve a depth of 20m if you so wish and the site can be dived at any state of the tide. The pebbly beach eventually turns to a sandy seabed the closer you get to the main bulk of the rocks. Depth wise, 10–15m is all you need here as it's all about that natural light. Although the biggest colonies of jewel anemones are on the overhangs, i.e. in the darker bits.

The tidal range here is impressive. Diving at high water means fewer stony steps to take over the beach with heavy dive gear before meeting the water (and when coming back again). Take a compass bearing before you leave the surface as the site is formed of several different rock formations, cracks and gullies. It is very easy to become disorientated — very easy indeed. Wade into the water, choose a section of rock to head for and submerge.

Lone-hunting John dory patrol here, cuttlefish too. If you keep one eye on the seabed it is possible to find solitary gurnard — a beautiful bottom-feeding fish that glides along on wings (pectoral fins) — that look like they could almost take flight. The kelp is a novelty for only a few minutes, soon wearing off, but the walls that meet the sand are where the creatures live. Between the rocks the gullies feel deep, shear and fun to swim between in single file, parting fronds of kelp and weed as one moves forward to reveal what lives within this space.

Angler fish (or "monkfish" as listed on the menu) are easy to miss but easy to pause by for much of a dive if you don't. With a lure positioned forward of their dorsal fin, these masters of surprise entice their prey into striking distance. Their markings and texture ensure that they are well-camouflaged against the similarly-coloured sea floor.

Drawna Rocks, as with most rocky dive sites in Cornwall is a habitat for the dazzling jewel anemone (take a torch) and white fluffy dead man's fingers (two a penny). Pollack, the occasional bass, ballan and corkwing wrasse all make regular appearances. During May and June basking sharks from time to time swim into the bay, trawling the water face first for food with gaping mouths.

Divers are more likely to find seals around the cove though. As well as hunting around the rocks, the usually solitary pinnipeds patrol the shallows picking off horse mackerel. These fish arrive here in huge numbers during the summer, just before sunset. Not quite at the bottom of the food chain, the mackerel in turn chase small bait fish up the pebbly beach, creating a frantic disturbance in the shallows all the way along the cove. This in itself is a wild snorkelling experience, but if on scuba and you end up away from the rocks in the early morning or late afternoon look up to the surface and you may see a cloud of mackerel passing overhead.

Porthkerris Divers' shop and air station is literally on the beach ... almost. They have two dive boats, two camping fields, a chalet rental and a snack bar. UK diving doesn't get much more convenient than this, Cornish coves don't get much prettier and camping doesn't get much cooler.

- Can be dived at any state of the tide. High water saves a longer walk to the entry/exit.

- The rocks are at the northern end of the beach.

10–18m

JEWEL ANEMONE-ENCRUSTED ROCKS

ANGLER FISH   ROB ROSLYN

BAITFISH CHASED ASHORE

MANACLES REEFS
50°02'40.63"N 5°02'46.18"W

YELLOW STAGHORN SPONGE

Off the eastern side of the Lizard Peninsula, on Cornwall's southern coast lies the Manacles Marine Conservation Zone (MCZ). These treacherous rocks, some of which barely break the surface at low tide, comprise Vase Rock, Raglan Reef, Carn-du, Pen Wyn, and The Voices. It is several dive sites in one maze of rock, reef, wreckage and kelp forest. The Manacles MCZ is renowned for its fast-flowing tidal currents and clear waters, supporting a broad range of marine life.

Raglan Reef is the outer most point of the Manacles and comprises a 5–45m steep pinnacle. Jewel anemones are found in great quantities on the north-east face and the wall glows like a packet of highlighter pens under torch light. Pen Wyn pinnacle descends from 6m to beyond 35m and features some stunning colourful sheer walls and cracks bursting with life. Vase drops from 10m down to 42m in several sponge, coral and anemone-coated tiers and gullies. The Voices (Maen Voes on the chart) which breaks the surface at low tide, is beside the final resting place of the *Mohegan* and so can usually be visited when shallowing-up from that wreck dive.

Plumose anemone forests populate the pinnacles and fish life is prolific. Ballan, cuckoo and corkwing wrasse, plus goldsinny make up the bulk of fish species. In deeper water on the many ledges, ling, dogfish, John dory, striped mullet and angler fish can be sighted. Another familiar "face" of UK diving and one prevalent here is the dead man's finger (*Alcyonium digitatum*). Members of the coral family, they thrive in great clusters populating both rock and wreck. Off the Cornish coast it is more common to find colonies of the white variety, with the orange more prominent the further we travel north.

Pincered common lobsters are distributed about the Manacles and spiny lobsters inhabit the reef also. Also called crawfish, crayfish and rock lobster, they are rare in water shallower than 20m and now a Priority Species due to a decline in numbers. Having made a comeback here though, it is easy to identify them — they have tiny claws rather than big pincers, are orange and brown in colour, sport antennae longer than their bodies and have spines on their carapace.

Another orange-bodied creature found on the reef is the seven-armed star fish. It is a surprisingly "quick" mover in starfish terms. It eats other starfish, urchins and brittlestars, while feeling its way through this watery world. Splashes of yellow pop from the rock in the form of sponges and pink sea fans stand on the reef where the currents flow.

These cold water corals create a wonderfully exotic display for the diver, especially when grouped together. A gorgonian sea fan species that is said to be restricted to south-west England and south Wales, they grow extremely slowly — at a rate of around just one centimetre per year. It is thought possible that some of the larger examples may well be over 100 years old. This delicate species is protected by the Wildlife and Countryside Act.

The shallow reaches of all of these rocks, whether Vase, The Voices, Raglan or Carn-du sport a mop top of kelp that flows back and forth as the water moves through it. This is not a comfortable place to be for a diver prone to motion sickness.

At the end of a dive, you will need to deploy a surface marker buoy at the Manacles, as there can be many boats around and strong currents. Take a torch to expose some of the creatures living within those cracks and caves. Aboard the boat, or even in the water if luck is with you, the animal encounters may continue further. Common, bottlenose and Risso's dolphins are regularly sighted with fin and even humpback whales spotted off the Cornish coast too.

🕐 Slack is +1hr HW/LW Falmouth. Vase should only be dived on slack on springs.

📍 Raglan 50°01'36.1"N 5°01'31.0"W
Penwin 50°01'43.0"N 5°01'27.1"W
Vase 50°01'46.3"N 5°01'25.4"W
Voices 50°02'43.2"N 5°02'36.0"W
Ten minutes from Porthkerris by boat.

DEAD MAN'S FINGERS

SPIDER CRAB AND PINK SEA FANS
DAMIAN BROWN

0–45m

SS MOHEGAN
50°02'43.2"N 5°02'36.0"W

ANCHOR　　　　　　　　ALEX GIBSON

SEVEN-ARMED STARFISH

Amongst the rocks there is some wreckage to explore here too, but by no means is it boat shaped. Along with a navigational error, Vase Rock and The Voices are the two other key components culminating in the demise of the *Mohegan*. On 14 October 1898, heading for New York on just her second voyage, the steamship broke her rudder on Vase before crashing into The Voices and sinking at 7:04 pm.

The 7,000-ton Victorian vessel previously named the *Cleopatra* was built by Earls of Hull. On her fatal voyage she was carrying a general load of beer and spirits, with animals as deck cargo. Of her 197 passengers, 106 lives were lost and a cross marks the victims' burial site at the churchyard in the nearby village of St Keverne.

Today, the wreck of the *Mohegan* is cast over a large area and depths on her range from 15–30m. She lays across the seabed and rocks in a north to south direction, minus the rudder of course which was dismembered during the initial collision at Vase. The massive boilers forward of the engine are the most notable attraction and a good point to start the dive. Having been extensively salvaged, much of this area has been left an indistinguishable debris field of collapsed plates, girders and gnarled metal. Other parts still appear in grid formation, simplifiying exploration, and rising above the wreck there gives a good sense of the scale of this ship. A keen eye is required to distinguish her former working parts, yet what looks like a prop shaft stands out from the chaos at the stern.

Among the metal, cracks in the rock and caves draw the diver closer, these areas now a habitat for marine flora and fauna. Nudibranch slide among the melee and hydroids can be found here too, while pollock in good numbers find shelter here also. The striking male cuckoo wrasse appear particularly inquisitive in these parts, keen

A DIVER INVESTIGATES THE BOILERS — ALEX GIBSON

on their own reflection in a diver's mask or camera lens port. The wreck has become fused with the reef, an extension of what was already there, creating yet more cover for creatures to call home.

- 🕒 Slack water is at +1hr HW/LW Falmouth and is imperative as currents are strong here. The dive often ends as a drift across the Manacles.

- 📍 Ten minutes from Porthkerris by boat. The boilers are about 50m east of north-east from Maen Voes (coordinates given above).

DIVER AT THE SURFACE

15–30m

FACT FILE

GETTING THERE Porthkerris is on the eastern side of the Lizard Peninsula — the most southerly point of mainland Britain — south of Helston, Cornwall. Head for St Keverne and turn left at the square. Be careful to follow signs rather than satnav once you're on the Lizard as some unhelpful detours have been known, especially for anyone towing anything!

ANYTHING ELSE? Divers shoulder cylinders to and from the filling station all day through the summer, the hiss of the compressor audible confirmation of this place's seasonal success. Regardless of how one chooses to dive here, when the dry suit has been hung up after a day spent exploring these ravishing south coast reefs, this is the place to switch off electronic devices and gawp out to sea instead.

DIVE OPERATIONS

Porthkerris Divers ferry divers by boat to the Manacles and elsewhere from their dive centre by the beach. At the time of writing, two boats are operated — one a small shuttle servicing dive sites considered local and the other, a larger catamaran more suitable for larger groups and locations further afield. Launching of one's own boat is possible from the cove too, with dive centre tractor support. Also supplied are air fills, complete kit-hire, accommodation, camping and a beachside snack bar — www.porthkerris.com
Atlantic Scuba, Penryn — atlanticscuba.co.uk also serve the area with boats out of Falmouth.

SPINY LOBSTER — ALEX GIBSON

JEWEL ANEMONES

ROCK
by Stuart Philpott

The fishing village of Rock sits on the north-east bank of the River Camel estuary on the north Cornish coast. This is a sheltered strip of water which meets a generous length of sandy beach topped with dunes. On the opposite bank of the river we find the equally posh holiday town of Padstow. Both places are of a certain pedigree and considered by some to be their Kensington by the sea. More importantly and with pretentious titles set aside, most of this area has been declared an Area of Outstanding Natural Beauty. The estuary is a sea bass conservation zone and is also home to one of the UK's rarest amphibious mammals, the otter.

Rock's dive centre community award their examples of upright wreckage and reefs five stars. Yet the north Cornish coast can be overlooked by those divers heading

RIVER CAMEL JOINS THE SEA

straight for the Mannacles reef, Drawna Rocks and the James Eagan Layne to mention a few southern classics. With Newquay on the periphery, this north coast location is primarily considered more of a surfer's hangout, with a greater share of wind and waves meeting these shores than can be expected of the go-to regions either side of Falmouth.

To bring the north coast back into the fold and to dissolve any kind of divide, here we explore two wrecks with Stuart Philpott where in-water visibility averages 10–15m, but can reach a whopping 20m. But being blown out owing to poor weather is possible with most UK sea diving locations, so let's not add too much gloss. At least in Rock, if that happens, then there is always Sharps Brewery to fall back on.

SS ANNA SOFIE
50°31'42"N 5°08'05"W

TRIPLE EXPANSION STEAM ENGINE

A World War I shipwreck lying off the Cornish coast made the local news headlines in 2019. There were two reported casualties when the ship went down, Private William Moore and an "unknown soldier". For nearly a century his gravestone had been inscribed "A Royal Marine of the Great War" but historian John Buckingham from Padstow Museum had finally revealed the true identity of the ill-fated soldier.

On 23 July 1918 the 97.5m long, 2,577 ton armed merchantman steamship *Anna Sofie* was "in ballast" (not carrying any cargo) returning to Wales. Without warning she was torpedoed by U-boat *U55* commanded by infamous Kapitänleutnant Wilhelm Werner. Between July 1916 and November 1918, *U55* completed 14 successful patrols sinking a total of 64 mostly unarmed ships (a total of 133,742 tons). The crew of around 70 including mortally-wounded marine gunner Private William Moore managed to escape in lifeboats and were rescued at sea. Nineteen days later the body of another marine gunner washed up on the shore at Padstow, badly decomposed. Unidentifiable, it was buried next to Private Moore with no name on the headstone. John painstakingly searched through the archives and discovered without any doubt that the unknown marine was Lance Corporal William Whitmore.

Even though the *Anna Sofie* is steeped in history she is not a popular choice with many divers and can be considered an "in-between" wreck. Recreational divers like to dive somewhere around 30m or less and it's too shallow for most techies. The *Anna Sofie* sits at around 43m max, tide depending.

Finds on the wreck over the last couple of decades have included a substantial number of brass shell cases, port holes and engine components. The aft gun manned by Lance Corporal Whitmore is yet to be found. The wreck is located in the middle of Padstow marine conservation zone. She sits right next to a reef wall and so it can be a challenge to find her for those not familiar with placing a shot on the wreck.

HEATING UNIT

Two large boilers, now the highest point of the wreck, stand 5m proud of the seabed. The four-bladed propeller and triple expansion engine (manufactured by Blair and Co) are also prominent, recognisable features. These areas are often loaded with colourful starfish and lobsters and conger eels peer from the darker recesses. The pointed bow has totally collapsed as has much of the surrounding superstructure.

If possible, pass close to the reef wall on the journey back to the shotline and if you find a number of antennae protruding from it, these will be crawfish (spiny lobsters).

If qualified, opt for nitrox 28 or a weak trimix fill, the latter being been the optimium option.

🕐 Slack water is essential, which is approximately +1hr LW/HW Newquay. But seek local guidance before diving in this area.

📍 On Harlyn Dive School's 8m RIB the 8.5 mile journey from Rock beach takes around 20 minutes.

38–43m

SS SPHENE
50°36'09.5"N 4°53'10.1"W

AN ARRAY OF STARFISH ON THE BOW

With a full cargo of coal, the steamship *Sphene* left Barry in South Wales bound for London. Heavy seas forced her to shelter behind Lundy Island in the Bristol Channel. A week later the ship continued on her journey despite unsettled weather. On the 5 February 1946 the 57m long, 815 ton freighter collided with the Mouls, a small offshore island mostly inhabited by cormorants. Initial damage reports confirmed she had been holed below the waterline on her starboard bow. The crew abandoned the foundering ship which ended up drifting one mile east-north-east of the Mouls before sinking upright in 23m of water. There was no loss of life recorded.

Today the SS *Sphene* wreck is found about four and a half miles off the coast and the local dive centre gives this site a five star rating. Visibility here is often in the 10–15m range but it can be as much as 20m. On the wreck, there are a number of rectangular-shaped openings along the starboard side. These openings are surrounded by multi-coloured spiny starfish and a huge shoal of silvery pollack usually fills the space too.

The *Sphene* still looks like a proper shipwreck with a recognisable bow and stern but there are no major penetrable areas. The mid section has all but collapsed and is mainly at seabed level. The three-bladed prop and rudder makes a great picture composition and this also happens to be the deepest part of the wreck.

There are starfish everywhere. Locals divers say that the site was once filled with fluffy plumose anemones too, but the starfish turned up and all the anemones disappeared. The stern is the most intact section, standing approximately 4m proud of the seabed. Pass over the top of the stern down onto the small quadruple expansion steam engine, this is another great photo opportunity. There are a few lobsters and conger eels lurking about the structure and several beautiful pink sea fans grow on the steel plates.

STERN

The bow is virtually intact except for a large gaping hole near the keel (which is probably the reason why she sank). It is said that the chain locker was ripped off by a fishing trawler and is now lying on the port side.

🕐 Slack water is essential which is approximately +1hr LW/HW Newquay. But seek local guidance before diving in this area.

👤 RIBs can be launched from a stretch of shingle/sand beach within the Camel Estuary. Harlyn Dive School have sole launching rights here, so contact them prior if using your own boat.

19–23m

THREE-BLADED PROPELLER

FACT FILE

GETTING THERE Rock is on the north Cornish coast about a 20 minute drive from Bodmin, more or less in the centre of the county. It sits across the River Camel from Padstein, sorry Padstow, from where boats can also be launched (concrete slipway alongside the Harbour Master Office).

ANYTHING ELSE? Newland Reef, usually a drift over dee gullies in the 15–20m range. *Caister* is a broken-up 1970s wreck in 14m max. *U-1021*, a World War II German submarine, but it is deep at 50m. If have time or are blown out, the National Lobster Hatchery at Padstow is well worth a visit. The estuary is the location of the notorious Doom Bar, a sandbar so treacherous it has a beer named after it.

DIVE OPERATIONS
Harlyn Dive School, Rock — www.harlyndiveschool.co.uk
Padstow Harbour Commissioners, Padstow — www.padstow-harbour.co.uk

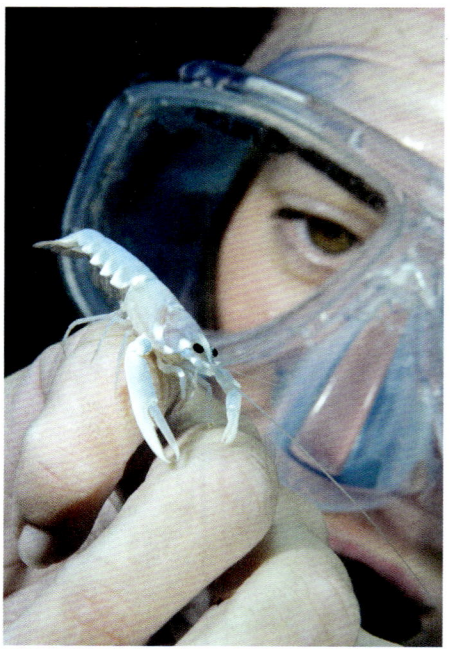

JUVENILE LOBSTER

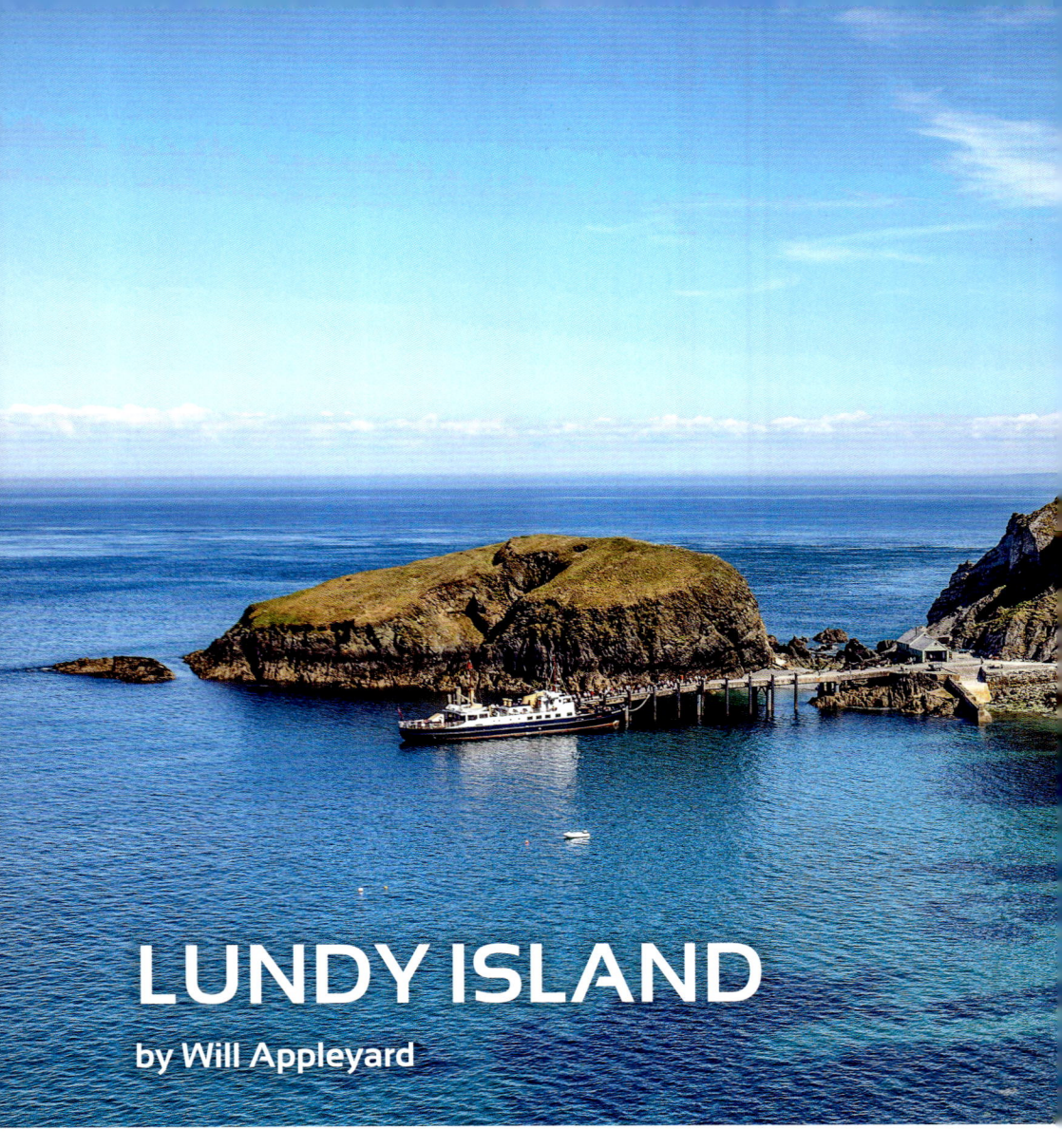

LUNDY ISLAND

by Will Appleyard

Lundy Island (Puffin island in Norse) is a difficult place to leave, emotionally. Physically too should poor sailing weather leave the explorer stranded there, perhaps gratefully so. This heathland-topped knob of granite is just three miles long and smidge over half a mile wide. Lundy sits in the mouth of the Bristol Channel and is licked by cool, clear Atlantic water. These ingredients mean that exceptional underwater visibility can usually be expected around the island, but by no means is this guaranteed.

Initially just a distant spec, this magical place feels further away than it actually is, slowly growing in size as the dive boat makes its approach. Devon becomes just a distant slither at the boat's stern. Once below the island's granite cliffs (some up to 120m high) and grassy slopes, everyday sounds from the mainland are replaced by those of

SOUTH END OF LUNDY

seabirds and the clank of readying divers and their gear. Puffins, gannets, razorbills and guillemots form a few of the winged regulars, with around 140 different bird species recorded as visiting the island each year. On the rocks at the base of the cliffs or rudely gawping from the water are one of several reasons to be here — grey seals.

In 2010, Lundy was the first area in England to be designated a Marine Conservation Zone (MCZ), created to protect nationally important marine wildlife, habitats and geology. There are no fewer than 40 dive sites around the island, with a handful of those being popular go-to points to explore, often in the east side lea. This special, remote island location is one of my favourite places to be, anywhere in the world and it is as much about simply being there as it is about the diving.

GANNETS' BAY
51°11'46.2"N 4°40'05.4"W

LUNDY'S GREY SEALS OFTEN MAKE WILLING SUBJECTS — DAMIAN BROWN

Lundy's grey seal colonies are distributed around most of the island. Gannets' Bay is the go-to place for divers and snorkellers to find them in the water, or hauled out upon the intertidal rocks. Around 60 seals form the breeding colony at Lundy, with twice as many present during the summer. Pups are born here in either September or October. Bulls live to somewhere in the region of 25 years of age and cows to around 35. On land these fin-footed pinnipeds are slow, heavy and cumbersome but in water they are big, powerful, wild animals. Once we have entered the sea, we have stepped into their environment.

The diving here is shallow, 10m at the deepest and the seabed a continuation of the rock shore. Dropping down the few meters to just above the kelp and weed, anticipation arrives. These feelings trigger twitchy looks in each direction, waiting for a finned figure to approach from the green. Look up to observe individuals floating vertically or "bottling" at the surface, but stay back respecting that the creature will come to you if it wishes. Sometimes they wish to stay away. An adult seal's generous size becomes apparent once the bulls make an appearance. Although the cows appear large too, the males can grow to in excess of 300kg and 3m in length.

Some like physical contact, but of course this always needs to happen only on their

FIN NIBBLING   MIKE DEATON

terms, never grabbing at or pulling the animal. The seal won't adhere to this rule of course. The grey seals at Lundy are beyond inquisitive and like to pay particular attention to a diver's fins. These whiskered, blacked-eyed seadogs investigate using their mouths in the main, tugging at neoprene, hoses, hoods and hands.

The Landmark Trust includes some obvious yet important points within their guidelines regarding seal interaction for divers and snorkellers: No feeding, avoid flash photography, no touching or chasing and keep your boat speed to a minimum to mention a few. But of all the diving experiences within this book, seal encounters must feature somewhere within the top five, perhaps even three. There are few large marine animals globally who are as keenly interested in us as we are in them.

Any state of the tide.

The faster, modern boats make the crossing from Ilfracombe in 60–90 minutes. Older craft take two hours.

0–10m

MV ROBERT
51°11'07.2"N 4°38'48.0"W

STARBOARD SIDE   TIM MOUNTJOY

The MV *Robert* was a diesel-engined German-built, Dutch-owned, Panamanian-flagged coastal trading vessel (coaster). She came to grief en route from Cardiff to Rouen in 1975 on the east side of Lundy Island, capsizing when her cargo shifted in heavy seas. The crew were rescued by the Croyde Lifeboat.

Now marked by a buoy, she is 50m long and lies on her starboard side. As sunken vessels go, this one remains ship-shaped — it is Lundy's only example of an intact wreck.

The outer hull is home to stalks of plumose anemone and nudibranchs. The guts of the *Robert*, at its former deck level, are a gloomy aquatic apartment block for conger eels, giant lobsters and shoals of bib. Most of this inner space, its one-time hold, is cavernous and open and it is possible to explore inside. Take a torch and avoid stirring up the bottom.

It is easy to navigate the *Robert* owing to its recognisable shape. She is a super fun wreck to dive, especially if one has already had their fill of grey seal attention. Under the bow at the seabed live swimming crabs, hermit crabs and scallops. The bottom is quite muddy and so the wash from a diver's fins will spoil the visibility if it is disturbed. The accommodation section of the wreck is navigable, but remain outside this structure. Manoeuvrable space for a diver inside is almost non-existent and like the seafloor, it is silty and easily disturbed.

It is possible to complete one, perhaps even two quick circuits of the site in one

FUNNEL COVERED IN ANEMONES, HYDROIDS AND SPONGES SIMON ROGERSON

dive, but really time should be spent examining the sideways superstructure in detail. More often than not there is ample natural light here, even down to seabed level at 25m. The exposed port side is found in 18m of water where the dive begins and a line should be in place, attached to the anchor winch at the bow to guide divers to and from the surface.

The wreck of the SS *Iona II* lies in close proximity to the MV *Robert*, but a license is required to dive that site so don't be tempted to pretend you "got lost".

Diving the MV *Robert* is only possible at slack owing to the fierce tidal currents present at any other time. The slack water window is quite accommodating though, being -2 to +2hrs LW.

1–2 hours from Ilfracombe by boat.

18–25m

FACT FILE

GETTING THERE Although not the only embarkation point for the island, Ilfracombe on the north Devon coast serves as a major hub for Lundy dive boat charters. The crossing is some 20 miles. Pods of dolphins are frequently sighted while at sea between the two locations.

ANYTHING ELSE? Managed by the Landmark Trust, the majority of the remaining buildings on the island are now renovated holiday rentals. Once homes, social, educational and working areas many of these properties date back to the 19th century. Examples include the Old School, Castle, Radio Room and Square Cottage to mention a few. There is a lighthouse atop too. Upon the island's plateau sits a small grassy camping field which, if staying on the island (and you should), accentuates a sense of expedition diving. The Marisco Tavern serves as the island's only pub and so naturally fulfils essential meeting room requirements for any dive team.

DIVE OPERATIONS
Obsession Boat Charter, Ilfracombe — www.lundydiving.co.uk
Easy Divers, Ilfracombe — www.easydiversnorthdevon.co.uk

WHO WILL FIND WHO FIRST? DAMIAN BROWN

A GREY SEAL
APPROACHES
MIKE DEATON

LLŶN PENINSULA

by Jake Davies and Will Appleyard

The Llŷn Peninsula in the north-west of Wales feels wild, green, rugged and remote. Underwater, the shallow bays, coves and stretches of sand that meet this finger of land are a reflection of these traits above in a miniature, more delicate form. Much of the peninsula is designated an Area of Outstanding Natural Beauty (AONB). Modest mountains, long extinct volcanoes and grassy hills stand over miles of pristine beaches, some considered to be the very best in Wales. Iron Age forts and coastal castles meet neat Victorian terraces within 84 miles of the Wales Coast Path wending its way around this lean piece of land.

Coves reach around the wild sea like the embracing earthy arm of mother nature, assuring safety and sanctuary against the full force of the sea for the marine life

AERIAL VIEW OF PORTHDINLLAEN

sheltering inside. Local marine biologist Jake Davies chooses this peninsula as his favourite place to explore our wild and temperate seas. Although it is not a high profile destination in UK diving circles, it must be considered an important one. Professionally and recreationally, Jake spends his time searching for and documenting what lives within the peninsula's globally-important seagrass meadows. Here, he raises awareness of some of the sea's little guys — the tiny bobtail squid, juvenile thornback rays and the stalked jellyfish.

   These quiet, out-on-a-limb sites could almost have been built for the shore diver and I am certain that, for much of the time, Jake has these nutrient-rich, mini-ecosystems to himself.

PORTH YSGADEN
52°54'15.7"N 4°38'55.1"W

SMALL SPOTTED CATSHARK

Situated on the north coast of the Llŷn Peninsula is the narrow sheltered bay of Porth Ysgaden (Bay of the Herrings). Heading down the dusty, narrow lane you'll see the ruins of a house and chimney situated on the headland before you. Running east to west there are rocks which extend out creating a natural breakwater for the bay and an easy site for every level of diver.

From the parking area a concrete slipway provides simple access down to the site entry on the sandy beach. The benches next to the car park are obvious and convenient areas to kit up. Access to the water is a short walk down the slipway, where on high water you can carry out final checks before navigating through the boulders. At low water however, the northern wall of the bay is a more suitable spot.

Heading out along the northern rocky wall or against the south-eastern rocks beneath the cliffs will mean diving amongst dense kelp and boulders. These kelp forests support a wide range of species which live between and on the fronds themselves, such as the flat shell (*Gibbula umbilicalis*). A variety of wrasses weave about the canopy. Lesser spotted catsharks (*Scyliorhinus canicula*) are seen either swimming or resting along the walls. Egg cases (mermaid's purses) can be found attached to the bases of kelp and sea oak. Nose into the crevices and caves along the walls and you will find some of the bay's smaller inhabitants like the tompot blenny, common prawn and, in the deeper parts, leopard-spotted goby. Look carefully close to the walls for well-camouflaged fifteen-spined sticklebacks (*Spinachia spinachia*), particularly at the shallower end of the bay.

Away from the wall towards the middle of the bay, the habitat changes, becoming sandier and dominated by bootlace weed. Plaice, flounder and spider crabs are seen here. Bull grey seals appear around Porth Ysgaden and lone individuals have been known to sneak up on divers.

Following the wall to the north-west, the rock opens into a series of gullies surrounded by tall kelp fronds that in turn lead us to the outer edges of the bay. The current can be strong as we leave the lee, making it difficult to navigate back through the gullies, so if you start to feel it pull it is time to turn around.

On the B4417 heading south from Tudweiliog, take the right after leaving the 30mph zone which is signed "Penrallt Coastal Campsite". Continue straight ahead when the road takes a sharp left. Pass the white house and take the next left into a narrow lane, which becomes a dirt track. Follow to the end.

During summer the slipway can be busy with boats, an SMB is recommended. The rocks are also popular with anglers, so carry a dive knife.

PORTH YSGADEN

FIFTEEN-SPINED STICKLEBACK

FLAT SHELL IN THE KELP FOREST

0–10m

CRICCIETH BREAKWATER
52°55'02.1"N 4°13'49.9"W

ENTRY POINT

The breakwater at Criccieth, Tremadog Bay, is overlooked by a ruined 13th-century castle on the rocky headland above. Criccieth Castle was built by Llywelyn ap Iorwerth (Llywelyn the Great) who was a prince of Gwynedd. Looking across the bay from the breakwater gives unobstructed views of the Cambrian coastline and Snowdonia mountain range. Throughout the Victorian town there are plenty of independent places for refreshment. Just up the hill from the breakwater is "Cadwaladers", a café famous for ice cream.

Parking is possible next to the breakwater, but arrive early to secure a place. Ensure that access to the slipway isn't blocked because this is used by both the lifeboat and for general launching. Entry should be made in the corner between the breakwater and the headland where there is a small concrete ramp between boulders. Avoid swimming close to the breakwater as it is popular with anglers. For your own safety, deploy a surface marker buoy and dive along the edge of the headland as you can expect boat traffic.

Swimming out, there are large seaweed-covered boulders which provide shelter for wrasse and goby species as well as shore crabs and prawns. The bottom then transitions into sand, where patches of seagrass can be found. Many burrowing species are camouflaged on or in the sand such as plaice, solenettes, dab and weevers. Be wary of weever fish — they have a venomous dorsal fin that can deliver a painful sting. More often than not you will see only their large eyes peeking out of the sand.

Small shoals of red mullet have been seen here by divers — they are normally found further south in the UK. Clumps of seaweed form havens on the sand for greater pipefish and common dragonet (*Callionymus lyra*). Many invertebrates can be seen, notably the

BLACK GOBY CAN BE FOUND PROTECTING THEIR BURROWS

worm-like pink sea cucumber, as well as sea potatoes and the necklace shell (*Euspira catena* or moon snail). This predatory mollusc prowls across the muddy sand looking for its prey. It also produces distinct egg capsules laid in an open collar shape formed from a mass of jelly and sand grains.

Due to the shallow nature of the site, it is also worth diving at night. Many of the species which stay buried or camouflaged by day can be observed hunting after dark. There is also less boat traffic then too.

NECKLACE SHELL

Opposite the lifeboat station, postcode LL52 0DN. Unload your gear and park along the promenade. Do not block access to either slipway.

Best dived at HW, when max depth reaches just over 5m. Further out, 10m is achievable but don't stray into the boat lane.

0–10m

GIMBLET ROCK
52°52'53.5"N 4°24'00.1"W

THORNBACK RAY

BLACK GOBY

EUROPEAN PLAICE

Half a mile past the eastern end of the promenade at Pwllheli is Gimblet Rock (Carreg yr Imbill), the remains of what was a granite quarry. The long sandy beach lined with sand dunes looks out to Cardigan Bay and the St Tudwals islands. Bottlenose dolphins can be seen passing close to shore when feeding around the harbour entrance.

A yellow marker buoy 200m off shore marks the location of an outfall pipe and dive site, so it is commonly used by divers as a bearing to head out on. Around the pipe there are large concrete mats, which are home to lobsters and crabs.

From the car park, entry to the water is a short walk over the sand dunes along the pebbly beach. Gimblet Rock itself is a perfect location to carry out final checks. During the summer months the beach is busy with bathers, boat users and the rock is popular with anglers. Deploy a surface marker buoy for your own safety.

Swimming away from the beach, the habitat transitions from pebbles to sand, then to a mix of gravel and mud. When reaching the concrete mats by the outfall, the sediment becomes more viscous.

On the seabed, or just below its surface, flounders, plaice and weever fish can be seen. One of the favourite species found here is European plaice (*Pleuronectes platessa*) with their bright orange spots. Various goby species are common, one of the larger ones is the black goby (*Gobius niger*) which is inquisitive — it will come and investigate divers.

It is possible to see thornback ray (*Raja*

COMPASS JELLYFISH

clavata) pups here. This is rare indeed on any UK dive and they are extremely well camouflaged. Currently, this ray's conservation status is "near threatened". Thornbacks like shallow sand, mud, pebbles and gravel, so this area produces perfect nursery conditions. A single female can lay up to 170 egg cases a year, and they are an important food source for many other fish species too. The rays move off into deeper water during autumn and winter, returning to the shallows in the spring.

Compass jellyfish (*Chrysaora hysoscella*), so named due to the distinct pattern on their bell, often drift by. It is best to keep some distance as they have long stinging tentacles which they use to catch prey.

Head towards the Gimblet Rock Holiday Park, Pwllheli, LL53 5AY — the car park is on the right just before the entrance, opposite the sailing club.

It is best to dive at HW, which reduces your walk with gear over the pebbles. There is usually little current at this site.

0–8m

PORTHDINLLAEN (SEAGRASS MEADOW)
52°56'41.4"N 4°33'46.7"W

LOOKING SOUTH TO OYSTER ROCKS

BALLAN WRASSE (LABRIS BERGYLTA)

Nestled away within a sheltered bay on the northern side of the Llŷn Peninsula is the fishing village of Porthdinllaen. The headland features the remains of an Iron Age fort. It then stretches out into Caernarfon Bay which looks out to the Eifl Mountains in the east, Holyhead to the north, and on a clear evening the Wicklow Mountains are visible to the west.

Access to the village by vehicle is limited to residents only. Walking takes 20 minutes through the Nefyn & District Golf Club course or along Morfa Nefyn Beach. Once at the village, you'll first see the iconic red bricks of the Tŷ Coch Inn situated on the beach front. This has been voted one of the top ten beach bars in the world. Pop into the pub, it's a traditional Inn and rammed with local maritime historical artefacts.

So, owing to the aforementioned access limitations and boat traffic during summer months, despite starting just off the beach this is definitely a boat dive.

At low water, the shallowest grass is visible. This meadow is one of the largest and densest of its kind in Wales and is estimated to be the size of 46 football pitches. It extends from the village shore to the outer edges of the moorings. Seagrass habitats are globally important, supporting an extensive range of biodiversity. They form a nursery for fish species and absorb carbon dioxide. In addition, the meadows produce oxygen, cycle nutrients, filter pollutants and have the ability to reduce wave energy.

Seagrass meadows are perhaps the most under-appreciated of all of the marine habitats anywhere underwater. But really, this isn't grass at all. It bears a resemblance to grass of course, owing to its appearance but its closest relatives are actually orchids and lilies. Much of the meadow at this location is dense and towards the end of the summer the bright green shoots can be tens of centimetres high. This creates more of a challenge when seeking out some of the inhabitants ensconced within their miniature forest world — but this is why they choose to be here.

Shoals of sand eels swim over the seagrass and two-spot gobies are common visitors in the upper reaches. Although they quickly disappear into the seagrass when disturbed.

Among the meadow, one finds a range of special species like the rare stalked jellyfish. This is a bizarre marine miniature and an interesting macro subject. The stalked jellyfish's behaviour differs from most of their relatives as they live attached to seagrass, weed and rocks rather than being a free-swimming plankton species. These critters have pom-pom style features at the end of each arm.

Snakelocks anemones (*Anemone viridis*) are here too along with diddy, mysid shrimps. Wrasse and small-spotted catsharks are regulars, plus plaice, pipefish (the greater and the snake varieties) and the fifteen-spined stickleback. Away from the seagrass, where it meets the fucoids (a brown seaweed) and kelp, small shoals of bass are frequently spotted.

SNAKELOCKS ANEMONE

PIPEFISH   DAMIAN BROWN

Launch from the slipway in Morfa Nefyn, Pwllheli, LL53 6BY. The journey is a couple of minutes across the bay. In summer there are speed buoys and a four knot limit within the moorings. It's best to dive the outer edges of the moorings where there are fewer obstructions and less boat traffic, making it easier to keep an eye on your divers. If you decide to brave the 20-minute walk here to do it as a shore dive, entry is best made along the outcrops known as Oyster Rocks, on the eastern part of the beach — **52°56'30.1"N 4°33'55.2"W**. This and avoiding the peak summer months will mean less contact with boat traffic.

The hill is steep and as the tide goes out reveals soft sand where many have become stuck in the past. So it is best to launch at HW or organise a tractor to aid you (Marine & General Engineering, Tel: 01758 720472 / 07788 715020).

0–6m

FACT FILE

GETTING THERE The Llŷn Peninsula is in north-west Wales, south of Anglesey and west of Snowdonia.

ANYTHING ELSE? Pre or post dive, take a walk along the coastal path to visit Porthdinllaen Lifeboat Station to meet some of the crew. Tap into their knowledge and hear their stories of the surrounding coastline and the bay's rich history.

DIVE OPERATIONS
Chris Green, Tyn Rhos Mynytho, Gwynedd Pwllheli, LL53 7PS. Tel 01758 740712 (air fills only).
Anglesey Divers, Anglesey — www.diveanglesey.co.uk (air/nitrox, equipment sales and hire).
Marine & General Engineering — Tel 01758 720472 / 07788 715020 (Porthdinllaen tractor).

PORTHDINLLAEN LIFEBOAT STATION

LLŶN PENINSULA

ZOSTERA MARINA

RATHLIN ISLAND
by Alex Gibson

Rathlin Island is a truly wild place — a rugged, L-shaped landmass thrusting up out of the North Atlantic, on the edge of the Northern Channel, a few miles off Ballycastle, County Antrim. Sparsely-populated even by rural Northern Ireland standards, wildlife flourishes here. Rathlin is a Special Protection Area because of its rocky habitat, reefs, cliffs and caves, a Special Area of Conservation, and a Marine Conservation Zone. It is also a special place for divers with generally good viz, a wide range of marine habitats and high biodiversity (but don't panic there are wrecks here too). This place is washed by strong, unpredictable currents and incredible depths are achievable, so visiting divers would be well advised to seek the help of an experienced local skipper.

On secluded seaward cliffs and in the air around them, great masses of seabirds such

CHURCH BAY

as razorbills, guillemots, kittiwakes, herring gulls and Atlantic puffins can be found making a huge noise and plenty of guano. If you are lucky you may even see some of them underwater at shallow depths on a dive.

Between or after dives your skipper might offer you the chance to step onto the island. If so, you should just about find time to walk up to the East Lighthouse where in 1898 radio pioneer Guglielmo Marconi's equipment was used to send the first commercial radio communication. Or, if you can resist the après-dive lure of the pub, short strolls (in opposite directions) around the harbour take you to the visitor centre and museum, where amongst the shiny brass artefacts you will find items recovered from the SS *Lochgarry*.

NORTH WALL
55°18'13.4"N 6°16'34.2"W

DIVERS DESCENDING ONTO THE WALL

ANEMONE-COVERED SHEER WALLS

The northern side of Rathlin Island is home to a collection of reef dives featuring sheer walls, arches, caves, colourful sponges, anemones, kelp forests and inquisitive seabirds.

Although like most dive sites the sweet spot for marine life here is perhaps down at 15–25m, for those seeking depth there is a whole lot further to go, with some parts of the wall dropping well beyond 200m. Do make sure all your kit is clipped on and weights are secure before jumping in.

Off Derginan Point there is a sea arch at around 30m which is adorned with sponges and anemones and the rest of the dive does not dissapoint with an abundance of life and pinnacles. Around 50m north of the point itself there is the site known as the Gullies where you will find a 4m wide gully at around 25–33m.

Walls decorated with every type of anemone and sponge you can imagine drop off to unfathomable depths. Life here literally clings to the side of a sea mountain. Up in the shallows there are kelp forests to weave in amongst, with overhangs and further, more modest walls to discover. Where there are hydroids you will find nudibranchs, so this is a good hunting ground for macro lovers, especially earlier in the season.

The absolute highlight for me though is spending a safety stop at Guillemot Gully with birds dive-bombing our position in search of the fish they have mistaken our bubbles for. They zoom past at eye level, glancing sideways — maybe they think we're hiding their lunch, or are

GUILLEMOTS SPEED PAST

HEDGEHOG SPONGE

SPONGES AND HYDROIDS

NUDIBRANCH (FLABELLINA PEDATA)

they just curious? Either way, they keep on coming — hundreds of birds over an elongated 15-or-so minutes just hanging in the clear emerald green water.

🕐 The combination of incoming tides and steep underwater cliffs can result in strong up and down currents. Swimming away from the wall can reduce the effect of this, but can also expose you to stronger horizontal currents. Slack is at approximately HW Belfast.

📍 Coordinates given are for Derginan Point which is approximately 30–60 minutes from Church Bay or Ballycastle by boat.

10–200m+

SS LOCHGARRY
55°15'57.4"N 6°10'26.2"W

OBLIGATORY TITANIC MOMENT AT THE BOW

The SS *Lochgarry* was a former ferry which had been requisitioned during World War II. She played a part in troop evacuations from Dunkirk, even surviving bomb damage to make it back to England with over 1,000 troops. After this she was used as an Irish Sea transport as well as making trips to Iceland and the Faroes. It was between trips to Torshavn in January 1942 that she made her fatal voyage. Empty save for ballast and 50 souls she left Glasgow for Oban only to encounter poor weather. Setting course for the Mull of Kintyre the master expected to see the light there and continued at full speed, only to strike rocks just off Torr Head, Ballycastle, a little after midnight. The crew were ordered to shore up the damage but make ready to abandon ship too. Having misjudged their position, SOS calls and distress rockets were not heeded and around 5:30 am the master and chief engineer were the last to abandon ship, their lifeboat arriving at Rathlin Island around an hour later. It was then that they discovered around half their crew were missing, it later transpiring that their lifeboats had hit rocks and capsized — any survivors of that initial terror subsequently succumbing to exposure after making it ashore.

Now one of Northern Ireland's most popular dive sites, the *Lochgarry* lies upright in recreational depths, just off the south-eastern corner of Rathlin Island. Although showing signs of age and the ravages of the sea there is a lot to recommend this wreck. Some of the wooden decking is still visible but what stands out, fairly incongruously, is the patch of black and white tiles. This is just about all that is left of a bathroom which has disintegrated, although some porcelain bits and pieces can also be seen.

The forward hold might make a nice penetration were it not for the giant-sized chain blocking your path. This was put there by the Royal Navy to prevent anyone accessing the munitions below.

The triple expansion engine is exposed and the bow stands several metres proud of the gravel seabed, at which level the damage to the hull which did for her is all too evident.

- Strong currents so should only be dived on slack water: -2 hours LW or -3hrs HW Belfast.

- Approximately 500m east off the south-eastern corner of the island. The SS *Lochgarry* is a short boat trip from either Church Bay or Ballycastle.

32m

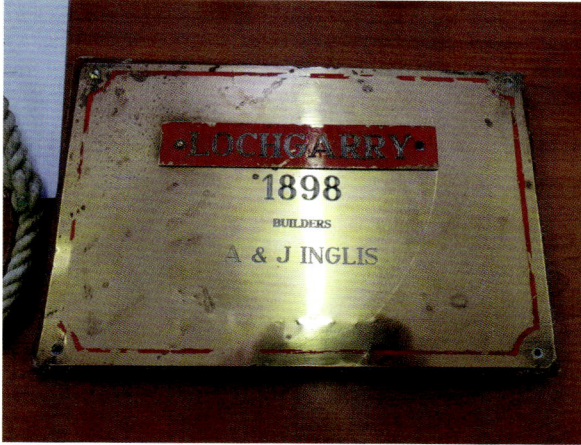
ARTEFACTS IN THE MUSEUM

BATHROOM TILES

DEVONSHIRE CUP CORAL

FACT FILE

GETTING THERE Rathlin Island lies just a few miles off the north coast of Northern Ireland. For those elsewhere in the UK, the shortest ferry journey is from Cairnryan, west Scotland, to Larne or Belfast. Other options include Birkenhead to Belfast, or via Wales and Ireland on the Fishguard to Rosslare route. Once on the mainland, smaller ferries can take you to Rathlin from Ballycastle, but you will need either your own dive boat or to be on one of Richard Lafferty's excellent charters. Given the complex currents in the area the latter is probably the best option for a majority of visitors.

ANYTHING ELSE? There are many other dives, including SS *Bouncer* (lost 1921), 6–8m — a British steamship with a propeller trapped under her boiler. Further afield even the deep wrecks off Malin Head are within range (from Portstewart) for the suitably qualified and equipped. If you are blown out then the Giant's Causeway is a short scenic drive along the coast and is conveniently close to the Bushmills Distillery, producers of Irish whiskey and the oldest licensed distillery in the world.

DIVE OPERATIONS Moorings are available in Church Bay but gas is not, so a return to the mainland for air is unavoidable.
Aquaholics, Portstewart and Ballycastle. Tel: 028 7083 2584 (air/nitrox, boat charters) — www.aquaholics.co.uk

RICH GROWTH HANGS FROM AN UNDERWATER ARCH

RATHLIN ISLAND

GUILLEMOT SAFETY STOP

FARNE ISLANDS

by Kirsty Andrews

The Farne Islands are a collection of uninhabited islands and rocky outcrops a couple of miles off the coast of Northumberland, split into the inner and outer Farnes by Staple Sound. The dive sites are mostly in the outer Farnes, a short boat trip from Seahouses. Depending on who you ask, the Farnes are famous for being a sanctuary for 7th-century monks including St Cuthbert, the scene of a fantastic rescue by lighthouse-keeper's daughter Grace Darling in 1838, a National Trust-owned haven for 100,000 breeding seabirds, or a hotspot for diving with one of the UK's biggest colonies of grey seals.

On the trip to the dive site it's worth keeping an eye out for dolphins and porpoises. You'll also see plenty of birdlife, especially in breeding season. Gannets are common throughout the year and puffins and Arctic terns are also numerous between April and late July.

LONGSTONE LIGHTHOUSE

After a diving day, there's usually time to visit the islands again by boat, this time to appreciate the nesting seabirds from above the water. Alternatively, visit the beautiful sandy beach and castle at Bamburgh for a lovely walk with a view of the islands from the shore. In fact, Northumberland has more than 30 miles of beaches and more castles than any other county in England — as you might expect from its strategic position close to the Scottish border. From Bamburgh to the Holy Island of Lindisfarne to Alnwick Castle and Garden, there are so many points of interest locally that the Farnes makes a great location for a mixed trip or a family holiday with a bit of excellent diving included. For a bit of variation you can also make your trip a double-header and spend a few days in the St Abbs and Eyemouth Marine Reserve, only an hour up the road.

SEALS
55°38'49.2"N 1°36'52.0"W

INQUISITIVE SEALS

LION'S MANE JELLYFISH

The topography of the Farne Islands is relatively consistent: kelp-laden shallows give way to steep rocky walls covered in dead man's fingers, down to a depth of around 15–20m. There are many sea urchins and the occasional lobster and passing jellyfish. It's a great location for novice divers due to the relatively shallow depths and of course the instant attraction of the grey seals. There are several individual diving sites within the Farnes themselves, such as the Hopper, Blue Caps, Big Harcar and the Longstone End (the coordinates given here). It's often wise to stay flexible and your skipper will select the best site on the day to provide shelter from the prevailing winds and tides and the best chance of seeing the seals.

The UK is home to 40% of the world's grey seals. The Farnes has a resident population of several thousand and is one of the most reliable places to see them. Seal pups are born in the late autumn and adolescent youngsters are particularly playful with divers so a good time to see them is around September, although encounters can be had throughout the year. The playful pinnipeds put a smile on any diver's face. They are often a little shy at first but like to sneak up behind divers and tug their fins. Once their curiosity has been aroused they often come back for another look, although divers should make sure that all interactions are on the seal's terms and that seals who have hauled out to rest on land are not disturbed.

If you're lucky, on your safety stop, you may get curious seabirds coming down to have a look at you, the intruder in their hunting grounds. From guillemots to razorbills to shags to occasional puffins,

GREY SEAL (HALICHOERUS GRYPUS)

the Farne Islands are one of the best places in the UK to see seabirds underwater. The best time for bird sightings is spring to early summer, when the birds flock to the Farnes for breeding season.

There is also no shortage of wreckage in the waters around the islands. Many are broken up and spread out but one of the most regularly dived and intact wrecks is the *Somali*, a World War II cargo ship sitting in about 30m. If you'd like to dive wrecks you'd be best advised to charter a full boat to control the itinerary, as most divers in the Farnes are in search of seals in shallower waters.

KELP AND DEAD MAN'S FINGERS

- High water is the best tidal state for underwater encounters as at low water many seals will haul themselves out onto the rocks to rest.

- Up to three nautical miles from Seahouses depending on site.

0–30m

FACT FILE

GETTING THERE Boats launch from Seahouses, 50 miles north of Newcastle.

ANYTHING ELSE? Snorkelling in the shallows with the seals is a good option for non-divers. In the autumn, pelagic RIB cruises are also available, searching for white-beaked dolphins and minke whales. You can search for cannon on the Gun Rocks dive trail — more info at gunrocks.co.uk. Make it a combined trip with diving out of Eyemouth or St Abbs, just 32 miles north.

DIVE OPERATIONS
Billy Shiel Boat Charters, Seahouses — www.farne-islands.com
Sovereign Diving, Seahouses — www.sovereigndiving.co.uk

PUFFINS ARE VERY FAST UNDERWATER

WHISKERS ARE VERY SENSITIVE FOR HUNTING FISH

ST ABBS
by Elaine Whiteford

St Abbs, Scotland, offers some of the best North Sea diving in the UK, its numerous sites part of a voluntary marine reserve that runs along the coast for five miles and extends, on average, a mile out to sea. The hub for diving is the picturesque harbour where you can park, get air fills and fill up with food at the excellent café. The short rides to the dive sites are an experience in themselves, as they offer close views of the sandstone cliffs and volcanic rocks that characterise the area. It's not unusual to see seals and dolphins en route and there are even a few minke whale sightings each year. In early summer, there are thousands of seabirds at St Abbs Head, including guillemots, razorbills, puffins, gannets and kittiwakes. And around the start of June, you can have some wonderful underwater experiences with curious guillemots.

ST ABBS, WITH ITS WILD SHORELINE AND A SKY TO MATCH

    The dramatic topside geology is mirrored below the surface, where there are steep walls, swim-throughs, gullies, stacks, and boulder reefs to explore. Most of the dives are scenic but there are also a few broken-up wrecks, the most popular being the *Glanmire*, which is scattered at 30m on a flat, sandy bottom.

    As befits a marine reserve, there is abundant and diverse sea life at St Abbs, including some species that are not routinely seen in the UK, like the Atlantic wolf fish and the Bolocera anemone. At most sites, there are distinct depth-related habitats, which offer excellent opportunities for multi-level diving and generous bottom times. You will get the most out of St Abbs if you are qualified to dive below 18m but it isn't essential, as there are plenty of sites where you can stay above that and still enjoy what's on offer.

ANEMONE GULLIES
55°55'12.0"N 2°08'38.0"W

YARREL'S BLENNY IN BRITTLESTARS

DAHLIA ANEMONE

If I had to pick one dive that offers the best all-round St Abbs experience, it would be Anemone Gullies. Situated north of the harbour, the site offers the chance to see classic St Abbs marine life in a stunning setting where almost every surface is covered in dead man's fingers, plumose and elegant anemones.

It's a 12–15 minute boat ride to the site and divers can be dropped in shallow or deep water, according to their dive plan. Twelve metres marks the top of the series of orange and white festooned rocky gullies which host a huge variety of crustaceans, fish, molluscs and nudibranchs. You can choose to dive along the top of the gullies or along their vertical walls (where you might spot a Wolf Fish in narrow cracks); or, you can swim along the sandy valleys near the seabed, losing count of the big common lobsters that loiter below the overhangs. I usually do a bit of all three as I zig-zag up and down.

The gullies end at around 23m, where there is a boulder reef with sandy pathways bordered by huge pink, yellow and white dahlia anemones, and where you can sometimes spot a curled octopus. As you go a bit deeper, you'll start to see expanses of common and black brittlestars, which completely cover the seabed by around 26m.

Heading back up to the shallows, keep an eye out for a camouflaged angler fish (monkfish) lying in wait on sand or rock. Although not always easy to spot, it is instantly recognisable, with its wide mouth, fringing chin and lure. I have found them very tolerant of divers and they seem to prefer to stay still rather than swim away. If they do swim off, however, you will get a glimpse of their dazzling white undersides.

Before putting up your SMB and ascending for your safety stop, spend some time exploring the kelp zone at around 8–10m, which is prime habitat for gobies, blennies and small scorpionfish, as well as nudibranchs.

Visibility at Anemone Gullies is usually among the best at St Abbs on any given day, and the north/south valleys in between the gullies give shelter from the current. If you only have time for one dive at St Abbs, make it this one.

Anytime — slack water not required.

Just a 12–15 minute boat ride from the harbour.

12–30m

DIVER EXPLORING THE GULLIES

CURLED OCTOPUS

ANGLER FISH

BLACK CARR
55°54'26.0"N 2°07'41.0"W

WOLF FISH

The wolf fish is undoubtedly the most iconic creature in the St Abbs marine reserve, and divers who spot one always gleefully report the experience once they're back on the boat. If your mission is to see a wolf fish, your best bet would be to head to Black Carr, just a five minute ride from the harbour.

The richest depth is between 17–21m, so get straight down and start your search. There is a knack to spotting wolf fish and, generally, you need to actively look for them. This means peering into cracks in the rocks, looking in the spaces between boulders and scouring dark crevices. A glance is usually not enough because, although you will sometimes see a wolf fish with its head sticking out of its lair, they normally position themselves a bit back from the entrance. Once you spot one, approach very slowly, preferably with your lights switched off, and the wolf fish will likely allow you to come close enough for a photograph. Despite their fearsome-looking teeth, wolf fish are placid and will retreat into their hole if uncomfortable with your presence; I have never seen one be aggressive to divers.

On a single dive at Black Carr, I have seen as many as eight wolf fish. Pairs in the same holes are not uncommon and, once, I saw three together. I can count on one hand, however, the number of times I've seen wolfies out in the open. So if you're lucky enough to see one out and about, keep your distance initially, as, once spooked, they can slither back to their hidey-holes in a flash.

The voluntary marine reserve conducts surveys of wolf fish sightings and divers are encouraged to use an app to enter the details. You can review the data online and see where the hotspots are.

Even if there were no wolf fish at Black Carr, it would still be a worthy dive site. A saying of mine for the many years I have been diving at St Abbs is that "there's never a bad dive at Black Carr". The site is a rocky reef with walls, gullies and flat boulder areas that are bursting with marine life. There are friendly ballan wrasse, which often follow divers around, lurking pollack and shy ling. It's also a good site for octopus and the deeplet sea anemone (*Bolocera tuediae*).

Black Carr has the same habitat zones as Anemone Gullies, and, after spending some time at depth, you can end the dive bimbling around at 10m exploring the vertical walls of the pinnacles, looking for small stuff amongst the anemones and dead man's fingers.

There can sometimes be a strong current at Black Carr, which can turn it into a lively drift dive, and surge is not uncommon in the shallows; but neither of these normally detracts from what is a top class site.

🕒 Anytime — slack water not required.

📍 A five minute boat ride from the harbour.

PINK PRAWN

BALLAN WRASSE

BOLOCERA TUEDIAE ANEMONE

12–30m

THE CRAIG
55°55'02.0"N 2°08'14.0"W

DIVER EXPLORING A PINNACLE

ANTIOPELLA CRISTATA

FJORDIA FEEDING ON HYDRIODS

ST ABBS: THE CRAIG

If Black Carr is the go-to site for wolf fish, then The Craig is the one to head to for the small stuff, particularly nudibranchs. Just a ten minute boat ride from the harbour, the site is located below the lighthouse at St Abbs Head.

It's best to get dropped off by the cliff wall to explore the inlets that are home to several species of nudibranchs, either on vertical walls or on the smooth stones on the seabed. There is a rich seam of sea slug life between 8–10m, where you can find, among others: *Fjordia*, *Polycera quadrilineata*, *Antiopella cristata*, and *Ancanthodoris pilosa*.

Once you've explored the inlets, you can head gradually down to a boulder reef, which flattens out to a sandy bottom at around 20m. There is less soft coral and anemone covering at The Craig compared with some others sites in the reserve so it can be easier to spot marine life, though not in great numbers, I have seen wolf fish, angler fish and octopus here, as well as the range of crustaceans and smaller fish which are common at most St Abbs sites. So even if you aren't a nudibranch enthusiast, this site offers an easy and relaxing dive, at depths that are accessible to divers of all experiences.

🕒 Anytime — slack water not required.

📍 A ten minute boat ride from the harbour.

12–20m

FJORDIA ON ROCK

ACANTHODORIS PILOSA

POLYCERA QUADRILINEATA

FACT FILE

GETTING THERE St Abbs is 50 miles from Edinburgh, 20 minutes off the A1. The postcode for satnav to get to the harbour is TD14 5PW.

ANYTHING ELSE? None of the three dives requires slack tide (unlike, say, the 30m deep wreck of the *Glanmire*) so there is no specific timing recommended. Skippers judge whether they are diveable based on wind, current and surge. They won't put you in if it's not the right conditions. When tides and sea conditions permit, there are a few dives directly from shore (including Cathedral Rock), but most sites are accessed by hard boat. There are three operators working out of the harbour and there is also a slipway where you can launch your own boat. Visibility is generally good by UK standards and can vary between dive sites: I have experienced 1m, 20m, and everything in between. Surge is not uncommon above 10m and some sites are prone to currents. There can also be surface swell, so SMBs are a must for every diver. Overall, St Abbs is a great destination, with more than enough sites to keep divers occupied for a week. Moreover, as there are plenty of activities for non-divers, it's an ideal place for a family break, too.

DIVE OPERATIONS Air fills are available at the harbour from Dive St Abbs, Rock House, St Abbs. Three boats operate directly from the harbour:
Shore Diver — www.divestabbs.com
Pathfinder — www.stabbsdiving.com
Stingray — stabbscharters.com

VELVET SWIMMING CRAB AND SAGARTIA ELEGANS

LOCH LONG
by Elaine Whiteford

Loch Long extends for 20 miles and is part of the Loch Lomond and The Trossachs National Park. The head of the loch is at Arrochar, which is a hub for other outdoor activities like climbing and walking as well as diving. There are places to stay and eat, and a petrol station. With several shore dives less than a 15 minute drive away, it makes sense to base yourself in the small town to explore the loch and its surrounds.

There is a large, but discreet, Ministry of Defence (MOD) presence in the area, both close to some of the dive sites and in the nearby glens, and you may see MOD police boats and Land Rovers out and about. In addition, there is an oil terminal on the loch and as Loch Long used to be a stopping-off point for steamers there are a few derelict piers dotted around. None of this detracts from the diving, though, as the

AUTUMN ON LOCH LONG

topside mountain scenery is impressive and past activities have created artificial reefs that are rich in marine life. Around Loch Long there are also good opportunities for land-based wildlife watching, with birds like heron, cormorants, oyster catchers and buzzards commonplace.

As with Loch Fyne, the shore dives at Loch Long are where there is relatively easy access to the water and enough space to park a vehicle safely. Because it is the closest diving to central Scotland, Loch Long can be busy at weekends with clubs and dive schools. However, on weekdays you're likely to have the sites to yourself and are guaranteed a dive at any time of year as the area around Arrochar is very sheltered, with negligible current.

FINNART (AKA THE A FRAMES)
56°07'02.0"N 4°49'49.0"W

A PAIR OF HARBOUR CRABS AMONG SEA SQUIRTS

This popular site on the east side of the loch can be reached from central Scotland in under an hour. Access is from a large surfaced layby close to Finnart Oil Terminal. There is frequently a very large tanker berthed 200m or so from where you enter the water and, if you look a mile in the other direction, you will likely see a grey aircraft carrier at the MOD Ammunition Jetty along the road. While this may not sound like the most prepossessing dive site, Finnart's hilly surroundings are spectacular and there is an extensive reef formed by the concrete support structures of a demolished pier.

The parking area is a couple of metres higher than the shore and care is needed going down the eroding rocky path. When the tide is in, the water comes to the side of the layby, while there is a short walk over small stones and kelp when it is out.

The reef's largest structures (the frames) follow the line of the shore starting at around 18m. All but one lie on their side and the top of the upright one (which looks like an A) is at 13–14m. They are covered in sea squirts, anemones, sponges, soft corals and hydroids, and home to all sorts of crabs — big edible crabs, aggressive velvet swimming crabs, skittish harbour crabs and delicate spider crabs. There are impressive clusters of peacock worms and on the surrounding seabed, Celtic feather stars and the tree-like

Psolus phantapus sea cucumbers. Finnart is also a good site for scorpionfish and dragonet, both of which are usually very tolerant of divers.

Start your ascent after the last of the big frames. As you swim up the slope, the structures are more broken up and the best depth for marine life is between 10–12m, where you can look out for gangs of common prawns and small groups of bivalve molluscs. When the debris peters out, head to shore and do your safety stop while looking on the kelp for nudibranchs, like *Limacia clavigera*. As Lion's mane jellyfish are often found in the shallows here, check that your way is clear before surfacing.

Finnart is a site that gets better the more you dive it and you'll get the most out of it if you go very slowly — there is lots to see if you look carefully.

🕐 Anytime — current negligible.

📍 The parking layby is on the A814, eight miles south of Arrochar. The postcode is G84 0EZ.

5–30m

ENTRY/EXIT POINT

LIMACIA CLAVIGERA

FEEDING PEACOCK WORMS

TWIN PIERS
56°11'40.0"N 4°46'17.0"W

CONGER EEL

This site is on the west side of the loch just under two miles from Arrochar and is easily identified by the platforms of two old piers not far offshore. A pavement runs alongside the road and there is a rough concrete area on the grass verge 40–50m from the site entrance where two vehicles can park. This is a busy stretch of the A83 and the traffic is both fast and close, so don't park on the grass or pavement. To reach the shore, go to the brick stage, then climb 2m down using the steel ladder that has been fixed to the wall by divers.

Once you reach the stony beach, the dive is an easy one and the gently sloping site straightforward to navigate. Start from the base of the platforms which, depending on the state of the tide, can be at anywhere between 2–4m. There are sea lemons on the barnacle-covered pier legs and large aggregations of mussels and starfish on the sand. It's worth poking around underneath the platforms as you'll find lots of gobies, crabs and whelks.

From the piers, go down to 15m and it's a straight swim left to get to the reef. En route you'll come across the remains of a fishing boat that is colonised by sea squirts, dead man's fingers and, early in the year, masses of whelk eggs which are feasted on by crabs.

LOCH LONG: TWIN PIERS

As you get closer to the reef, you'll start to see burrowing anemones and sea loch anemones carpeting the bottom.

The reef itself is made up of boulders, some of them very large indeed, covered in all sorts of anemones. Particularly attractive are the orange and white plumose anemones where long-legged spider crabs nestle.

Twin Piers is an excellent site for conger eels, although you have to hunt for them as like wolf fish they tend to hide in dark recesses. I have found the conger eels at this site to be quite curious and they will edge out of their holes to see what's going on. Squat lobsters and common prawns often share the lairs and, if you're trying to get a picture of a conger, your photograph might well be bombed by a small critter.

The reef runs from 8–30m and once you've fully explored it, head back to the platforms. I usually come off the reef and go immediately up to a stony strip at 5–6m where there are pipe fish in the kelp, queen and king scallops and lots of small fish and shore crabs. The strip runs all the way back to the entry point so just keep swimming until you reach the pier legs.

Anytime — current negligible.

By the A83 on the west side of Loch Long, just under two miles outside Arrochar. The postcode for satnav is G83 7AR.

4–30m

ACCESSING TWIN PIERS

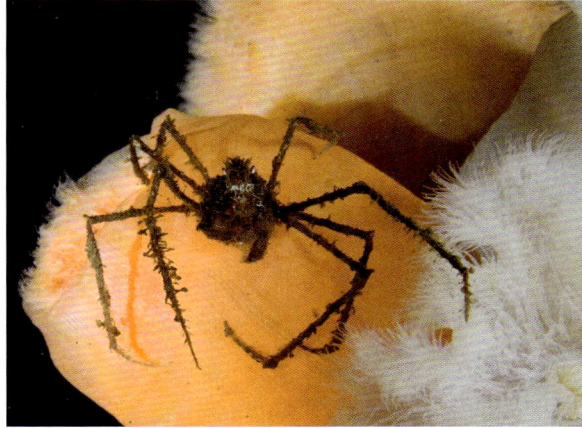
LONG-LEGGED SPIDER CRAB

GREATER PIPE FISH IN WEED

FACT FILE

GETTING THERE Loch Long is a sea loch off the Firth of Clyde on the west coast of Argyll and Bute, Scotland. Be careful not to confuse it with Loch Long in the Highlands. Postcodes and GPS are given for the dive site locations. Arrochar is around 40 miles north-west of Glasgow.

ANYTHING ELSE? Why not combine a trip here with diving nearby Loch Fyne?

DIVE OPERATIONS
Both sites are shore dives. The nearest air fills are in Glasgow (40+ miles). Aquatron Dive Cente, Glasgow — www.aquatron.co.uk

MALE DRAGONET

LOCH LONG

LION'S MANE JELLYFISH

LOCH FYNE
by Elaine Whiteford

If you like relaxed diving, with freedom to set your own timetable and to explore places that just take your fancy, then the sea lochs of western Scotland are for you. Formed by glaciers, these tidal inlets offer a variety of diving, much of which can be done simply by stopping at the roadside, kitting up and walking a few paces into the water.

Loch Fyne, at 41 miles long, is the largest of the sea lochs. Its head is just beyond the settlement of Cairndow, 50 miles from Glasgow and 96 miles from Edinburgh. Just before Cairndow, you can choose to explore either the east side of the loch or the west side: the west side has more villages, while the east is less developed and feels more remote. Both sides, though, offer shore dives that make a trip worthwhile.

You need to plan your excursion carefully to make sure you have everything you

LOCH FYNE, SET AMONGST ROUNDED HILLS AND WOODLAND

need with you. Air fills can be up to 50 miles away and there aren't any facilities (like car parks or toilets) at the dive sites; rather, there will usually just be a space by the shore for a few vehicles in a small layby, turn-off, or piece of rough ground.

Whichever rocky bay you dive from, you will be surrounded by gentle hills and, as such, the sites are well-protected, with little in the way of waves. Indeed, on still days, the water can sometimes be mirror-like. However, the sea lochs are tidal and there can be current, particularly at some of the more exposed sites. Given that Loch Fyne is such a large body of water, conditions vary from site to site. The topography includes rocky reefs, boulders, sandy seabeds and artificial reefs. Whichever site you choose, though, you will find plenty to interest you in quiet surroundings, well off the beaten track.

ST CATHERINES (FORMER COUNCIL YARD)
56°13'37.0"N 5°01'11.0"W

SQUAT LOBSTER AND FIREWORKS ANEMONE

St Catherines is on the east side of Loch Fyne and the dive site is just opposite the sign for the village. There is an unsurfaced piece of ground by the lochside which at the time of writing only has room for a single car as the rest of it is usually chained off. The shore is stony and at low tide there is a lot of exposed kelp, so it can be slippery underfoot.

Below the surface, the site slopes down extremely gradually and it can take you five minutes to reach a depth of 4m. The bottom is covered in lugworm casts, many of which have hermit crabs perched on top. As you descend, look carefully for brown prawns covering themselves in sand to hide from you and venomous lesser weever fish lying in wait for prey.

The main boulder reef is straight out from the entry point, starting at around 12m and extending to 25m. However, I find the most rewarding route here is via the expanses of sand to the left of the reef for some muck-diving, Scottish style.

Although at first glance this area of the site might appear barren, it is actually home to a great many creatures, some of which are uncommon. In the 12–15m zone, you will often see the strange sea mouse worm, with its iridescent pink, yellow and green bristles, and if you examine isolated clumps of weed, you will find common prawns and dozing dogfish. If you're lucky, you may see a thornback ray; and, if you're very lucky, a cuckoo ray.

By about 18m, the seabed is busier with swathes of fireworks anemones, which often have squat lobsters or crabs sheltering below their flowing tentacles. It is usually dim (sometimes dark) at this depth and as you scan the bottom with your torch, these large anemones stand out like beacons. Make sure you approach them gently, though, as they will coil back into their tubes at the slightest disturbance.

Continuing below 20m, you will start seeing lots of burrows in the sand. If you shine your beam down one, you will probably see the white-tipped orange claws of a langoustine. There is a large bed at this site and, if you are patient, you can watch these curious lobsters edge out of their burrows and, sometimes, go walkabout. Take care with your finning technique at this depth, as the bottom is extremely soft and clouds of sediment are easily kicked up.

You can either return the way you came, or head over to the boulder reef to explore for squat lobsters, crabs and nudibranchs. There is another small reef at around 6–9m, where you can finish the dive, doing your safety stop as you slowly head back to shore.

Anytime — current negligible.

St Catherines is on the eastern side of the loch, on the A815, six miles from Cairndow. The site is opposite the sign for the village. The postcode for satnav is PA25 8BB.

6–30m+

WEEVER FISH

SEAL REEF
56°12'38.0"N 5°03'18.0"W

SMALL-SPOTTED CAT SHARK

Although Seal Reef is just a mile and a half further along Loch Fyne from the Road Depot/Council Yard, it is a very different site. It is just off the A815, 100 yards along a no-through road, which you can park at the side of. To get to the water, you go down a banking using a set of makeshift steps constructed by divers. There is a rope tied to trees to hold onto.

Underwater, the site is much more compact than St Catherines. A gently sloping shelf goes down to around 4m, when the seabed then gets steeper, with a stony strip between 5–9m. You can either swim along this to get to the main reef, or you can go beyond it and swim over sand. Mostly, I go out over the sand and come back along the strip, where I also do my safety stop.

The main reef is made up mostly of relatively small boulders, with a few bigger ones under which cod, ling and common lobsters hide. It is crammed with small crustaceans and it's an excellent place to see three different types of squat lobster. The long-clawed squat lobster is numerous, but you will also see blue and red spiny squat lobsters as well as the smaller, more timid black squat lobster, which usually retreat from view as soon as you approach them. A thick steel cable runs through the reef at around 16m and is covered with sea squirts, peacock worms, anemones and spider crabs. Seal Reef is a good site for fish, with lots of little gobies and curious goldsinnies darting around.

BOBTAIL SQUID

You will also come across fifteen-spined stickleback, dogfish, and flatfish, like dab and topknot. If you visit in April–May, you will see many of the striking Fjordia nudibranchs, particularly around 14–15m.

It will be obvious when you reach the end of the reef as it stops abruptly, with a clear divide between the boulders and the sandy areas. It's worth having a mooch around the edges of the reef, as you can sometimes spot bobtail squid. I usually head up to the shallows at this point and swim slowly back to the entry point, keeping just above 6m.

5–25m

Seal Reef is an easy and relaxing dive; but there are two things to be aware of: 1) it's best avoided at the weekends as it's a popular training site for dive schools and clubs and; 2) don't be fooled by its name — you might see the occasional seal (usually at the surface) but it's not the Farne Islands!

The site is just over a mile and a half beyond St Catherines, where there is a turnoff from the A815 onto a no-through road. There is usually a large green refuse bin at the turn-off. Postcode for satnav is PA25 8BA. There is parking for around ten cars.

ANCHOR POINT
56°04'06.8"N 5°15'54.7"W

TWO SPOT GOBY WITH PREY

TRINCHESIA NUDIBRANCH

Anchor Point is a remote site on the east side of Loch Fyne, seven miles along a single track road and 21 miles from the head of the loch at Cairndow. Although it's not a quick trip, Anchor Point is an interesting dive and has a different look and feel to others along this side of the loch.

There is a small layby on the road above the site, with space for three or four cars, and a short grassy path down to the picturesque bay. Entry to the water is easy and the reef begins almost as soon as you descend the gentle slope.

The main reef is formed by an extensive rocky promontory that extends beyond 30m depth. You can dive along the top of the rock, explore the walls and also take in the sandy bottom. It is a very good multi-level dive and there is lots to see at all depths.

The top of the promontory and walls are covered in feather stars, sea squirts and hydroids, and you can spot lots of nudibranchs, including some fairly large *Polycera faroensis* and the colourful *Trinchesia caerulea*. This is also a great site for seeing the very large (to 12cm) *Pleurobranchus membranaceus* nudibranch which, like the Spanish dancer, can give an impressive swimming display. The walls of the promontory are tiered and there are lots of cracks, crevices and ledges which are crammed with lobsters and crabs. Anchor Point is also an excellent site for large echinoderms — the seven-armed starfish with its fringing arms can be seen, as can the attractive red cushion star and purple sunstar. The reef goes down to over 30m and if you drop onto the bottom there are groups of small boulders guarded by large congregations of long-clawed squat lobsters. On the way back to shore it's worth going off the reef every so often to explore the sand and kelp for molluscs and small fish, including the attractive two-spot goby.

Given its location, it makes sense to spend the day at Anchor Point and do more than one dive. Three is ideal as you can explore each of the plateau, the walls and the bottom.

LOCH FYNE: ANCHOR POINT

SQUATTIES

🕐 Anytime — current negligible.

📍 The site is on the B8000, which is single track (with passing places) for approximately seven miles. The postcode for satnav is PA27 8BU.

7–30m+

ANCHOR POINT SHORE ENTRY/EXIT

FACT FILE

GETTING THERE Loch Fyne is a sea loch off the Firth of Clyde on the west coast of Argyll and Bute, Scotland. It is 50 miles north-west of Glasgow and 96 miles from Edinburgh. All three sites are on the eastern side of the loch.

ANYTHING ELSE? Why not combine a trip here with diving nearby Loch Long?

DIVE OPERATIONS
All three sites are shore dives but Loch Fyne Dive Charters do run boats too.
Loch Fyne Dive Charters, Tarbert — www.fyne-diving.co.uk
Aquatron Dive Cente, Glasgow — www.aquatron.co.uk
Puffin Dive Centre, Oban — www.puffin.org.uk

NORWAY LOBSTER (LANGOUSTINE)

MULL
by Kirsty Andrews and Dan Bolt

The Sound of Mull is a focal point for divers in the west of Scotland, with good reason. Many ships have been attracted to this relatively sheltered route through the Inner Hebrides, but a large number have also sunk beneath the sea here. None of the three wrecks highlighted in this section were wartime losses; all fell foul of tricky weather conditions.

Divers looking to explore the Sound can choose to stay on the mainland, perhaps close to Lochaline, or take the ferry from Oban to Craignure, or Lochaline to Fishnish to stay on the Isle of Mull itself. Both options are convenient, but my preference is to stay on Mull and enjoy the beautiful island's scenery and wildlife.

Otters can be regularly spotted at dusk and dawn, hunting on the seashore, as well

TOBERMORY

as a host of seabirds. Mull has a healthy population of white-tailed sea eagles and golden eagles, and their regular haunts can be visited during a surface interval. Other highlights for a non-diving day include the beach and sculpture trail at Calgary on the north side of the island, and a climb up Ben More. This 966m peak is the only Munro on any of the Scottish islands except Skye.

Tobermory, formerly a fishing village dating back to 1788, is now a tourist attraction in its own right. The famous colourful frontage, immortalised in the children's programme Balamory, mainly now consists of tourist shops and cafes. Tobermory is often a good stop off in between dives, or indeed after diving groups may wish to visit the Mishnish pub or Oban Distillery in Tobermory for a whisky tour.

SS HISPANIA
56°34'55.7"N 5°59'13.0"W

EXPLORING A COMPANIONWAY

The *Hispania* is a wonderful, colourful corker of a wreck and has been drawing divers to the Sound of Mull for decades. Sitting in 32m of water with a deck level rising up above 20m, she is in ideal Sports Diver range but this part of the Sound is subject to fierce tides so I recommend a firm grasp of slack water times and a degree of diving experience to appreciate this classic wreck properly.

At just over 72m long she is a relatively small, steel steamship built in 1912 and sunk in December 1954 en route from Liverpool to Sweden. During a bad winter storm in terrible visibility she ran into Sgeir Mor ('Big Rock') reef in the Sound, which soon proved a fatal error. All of the crew escaped on lifeboats, but Captain, Swedishman Ivan Dahn, chose to go down with his ship. The *Hispania* sank quickly and some reports from the time suggest the crew saw their captain saluting from the bridge as she disappeared beneath the sea. Since the sinking the wreck has been thoroughly salvaged and has been wire swept to protect shipping, but despite this, there is lots to explore.

The *Hispania* lists slightly to starboard but otherwise feels relatively upright and intact, so is pretty easy to navigate and it is possible to circumnavigate the wreck and explore a little of the holds on one dive. Having said that, she's so pretty that you'll definitely want to come back and dive her again. Every inch is covered in plumose anemones, sponges and dead man's fingers, making her one of the "squidgiest" and most colourful wrecks in the UK. This abundance of life is due partly to the strong currents of course — make sure you don't overstay your slack water window.

The stern at around 30m is the deepest part of the dive and worth a look; although the propeller has been salvaged, the rudder and prop shaft are still in place. On the way across the wreck to the bow there are plenty of relatively open swim-throughs and five

ONE OF THE MASTS

holds to poke around in for those inclined to do so. The engine room is a little tight but the triple expansion engine can easily be seen. On sinking, the holds apparently contained plenty of steel, some lifeboat props and monofilament line, amongst other things, though I've never found any myself. The bow is at around 24m and still stands proud. Returning to the shotline, there is plenty to admire, from winches, derricks, impressive superstructures to the remains of the two masts.

SUPERSTRUCTURE AND PORTHOLES

- Slack is notoriously difficult to predict and more reliable on spring tides, it is at around -2 to -1hrs HW/LW Oban.

- Seven nautical miles from Lochaline.

15–30m

SS RONDO
56°32'18.4"N 5°54'44.9"W

DIVERS DESCENDING ON THE RONDO

The *Rondo* is an excellent introduction to diving the Sound of Mull. This is because she lies sloping gently on the reef wall with a very convenient profile from 3–4m to just a smidgen shy of 50m. Divers can pick their target maximum depth of anywhere within this range, confident that unlike most flat-profiled wreck dives, they will have something of interest to look at all the way to their safety or decompression stop. Depending on tides it does require a bit of grubbing around in the dirt to get beyond 49.9m and there's not much to see in the bow section down there, other than the magic number on your dive computer.

On the way up, the wreck is relatively narrow and I think of this site as a bit of an escalator of fun. It has been thoroughly salvaged leaving not many metal features of interest for the techie-minded but there is a good covering of wildlife, notably peacock worms all over the hull, and some interesting crannies to poke a torch into all the way up. The rudder post in 3–5m is absolutely full of soft corals and anemones to fascinate divers for even the longest decompression stop. There have been a couple of swim-throughs on the way upwards between the hull and the reef, but the 35m one has now mostly collapsed, leaving the 28m route the only current viable path under the *Rondo*, and that too may not last long. If you tire of the wreck itself then the reef wall is also interesting, full of feather stars, sea stars and kelp habitat.

The *Rondo* was built in America towards the end of World War I in 1917 under the original name *War Wonder 1*. She was renamed *Lithopolis* and in peacetime became *Rondo*. On her final journey on 25 January 1935 she was en route across the top of Scotland towards Northumberland to pick up cargo when she was forced to anchor near Tobermory due to a fierce storm. The storm proved so ferocious that her anchor chains broke and her crew were helpless as she drifted ten miles down the Sound of Mull until eventually hitting the north west shore of Dearg Sgeir near the lighthouse there. At first she was a boat out of water, so much so that her crew all stayed aboard for two weeks while various attempts were made to refloat her. Eventually it was decided that this was impossible and she was salvaged then gently drifted underwater on to the steep reef wall where she now lies.

Slack water is -1hr HW/LW Oban.

Her position is just four nautical miles from Lochaline.

5–50m

DIVER BELOW THE RUDDER

EMERGING FROM THE HULL

PEACOCK WORMS

SS SHUNA
56°33'26.0"N 5°54'52.0"W

PROPELLER

The *Shuna* is another upright, mostly intact wreck which offers a pleasing contrast to other Sound of Mull wrecks due to her sheltered location. The lack of current means there is a thick layer of silt settled on her so, although visibility can be a pleasing 10m, if other divers have recently been in and not taken care, this can be a murky dive. The silt also affects the wildlife that has settled on her. Unlike the more exposed *Hispania* and *Rondo*, the deck levels are relatively sparsely colonised, but by species which prosper in these conditions — tunicates, hydroids and notably, a healthy colony of northern sea fans. The bow is the most exposed section and this is well covered in plumose anemones and peacock worms, including the anchor which still protrudes through the hawse pipe.

She sits in around 32m of water with a main deck at about 25m and the superstructure coming up to 16–18m. Steps lead from the main deck level and there is an array of winches, masts and funnels to explore.

The *Shuna* sank on 8 May 1913 when, in poor visibility, she hit Grey Rocks at the southern entrance to the Sound of Mull. Captain Elsper tried to make for Tobermory, but, taking on water quickly, was forced to run her aground on the coast near Morvern. Only 200m from land, it is technically possible to visit the *Shuna* as a shore dive but I have not tried it and prefer the reassurance of boat cover.

She was left undisturbed for many years but rediscovered in the 1990s when divers stripped any brass artefacts from her. There is still coal to be found in her five holds, and neither the propeller nor the spare propeller on the stern deck has been removed. The engine room is worth an explore although it's difficult to squeeze past the triple expansion engine and this is an area to be particularly careful of silt. Her vital statistics are 1,426 tons, measuring 240.9ft by 35.2ft by 16.5ft and it's possible to circumnavigate

BRIDGE AND SUPERSTRUCTURE

this relatively compact wreck on one dive, or to take your time exploring the holds and deck areas over multiple trips.

- Diveable at any state of the tide.
- 200m from the shore near Morvern, nine nautical miles from Lochaline.

16–32m

CLUSTER ANEMONES

FINGAL'S CAVE (SNORKEL)
56°25'52.9"N 6°20'29.1"W

ANEMONE AND SPONGE LIFE

It is not often that you get the chance to snorkel in a unique geological feature, but Fingals Cave on the island of Staffa on the west coast of Scotland is just such a place. This 70m long sea cave is formed out of huge hexagonal pillars of basalt, created by cooling lava and subsequently eroded by wave action.

The journey to Staffa is stunning in its own right as the island lies around six miles to the west of Mull. Even from a distance this island looks odd, and as you approach you can see just how peculiar the tall hexagonal pillars look. It's hard to believe they're not actually man-made.

The cave is large enough to drive a decent sized RIB into, and at high tide is around 7m deep and 20m tall. It is very popular with day-trippers from Oban and Mull, who will walk around the island and into the cave. But being in the water inside the cave is a different experience altogether.

Swimming towards the cave, you will fin over fields of huge kelp and metres long thongweed (*Himanthalia elongata*) with some deep gullies and overhangs. There are plenty of wrasse and pollack here too. Heading into the cave and the seaweeds stop abruptly as the light levels drop off.

MULL: FINGAL'S CAVE

As well as the awe-inspiring view of the cave up-close, there is also a surprising amount of marine life to be found on the sheer walls of rock. Toward the entrance are many bright-red beadlet anemones and further in you'll find large numbers of white-and-yellow sandalled anemones.

More colour is added by the many species of encrusting sponge, with white, orange, green and purple varieties everywhere. It is definitely worth taking a torch with you to see their true colours.

A little way to the north from the main cave lies a smaller one, which is well worth the swim to go and explore further.

APPROACHING STAFFA ISLAND

- March to October, but the sea needs to be calm to enter the cave, as any sort of swell can make for difficult snorkelling conditions.

- Staffa lies about six miles to the west of Mull. Get there with operators who run boat trips from Oban and Mull.

7m

BASALT PILLARS

SNORKELLERS IN THE CAVE

FACT FILE

GETTING THERE The Isle of Mull is in the Inner Hebrides. The Sound of Mull lies between Mull and mainland western Scotland. It is possible to choose where amongst these incredible surroundings to stay and be collected by your dive boat each morning. Salen is my personal favourite, with its own private pier. Boat launch sites include Tobermory on the Isle of Mull, Lochaline and Oban. Charters run from Lochaline and Oban.

ANYTHING ELSE? For a break from wreckage, the Calve Island wall is beautiful and dramatic. Other excellent local wrecks include the *Thesis* (12–35m) and *Breda* (10–25m). If conditions allow, venture outside the Sound towards Coll and Tiree for potential wildlife encounters with basking sharks and minke whales and more wrecks in often very clear water.

DIVE OPERATIONS
Lochaline Boat Charters, Lochaline, Morvern — www.lochaline-boats.co.uk (also gas)
Puffin Dive Centre, Oban — www.puffin.org.uk
Basking Shark Scotland, Oban — baskingsharkscotland.co.uk

MULL WRECKS by Kirsty Andrews.

FINGAL'S CAVE by Dan Bolt.

SNORKELLING AROUND STAFFA

SHUNA BOW

SCAPA FLOW
by Jason Brown

"Paragraph Eleven, confirm". These seemingly innocuous words marked the beginning of an extraordinary chapter in naval history that to this day fascinates divers and historians alike. At 10:30 am on 21 June 1919, Admiral Ludwig von Reuter issued the coded order that lead to the scuttling of the German High Seas Fleet which had been interned at the end of World War I in Scapa Flow, Orkney.

As the Royal Navy looked on helplessly, one of the world's most potent naval fleets engaged in a last act of defiance on a grand scale by simultaneously opening seacocks and smashing pipes, sending 52 vessels to the sea floor. As the years passed, all but seven of the vessels were raised in what became one of the most audacious salvage operations in history. Those that remain beneath the waters of Scapa Flow continue to draw divers

CALF OF CAVA LIGHTHOUSE OVERLOOKS THE AREA WHERE THE WRECKS RESIDE

from around the world who want to see the surprisingly intact evidence of one of the most dramatic events of the war.

Scapa Flow is a vast natural shallow-water harbour within Orkney, an archipelago approximately ten miles off the most northerly point of Scotland. Wild and windswept, the islands are breath-taking in their natural beauty with tall sandstone cliffs, ancient stone circles and sea stacks that break through the churning blue waters.

A visit to the Scapa Flow Museum on the nearby island of Hoy is a must. Featuring artefacts recovered from German and British wrecks spanning both World Wars, it provides a fascinating insight into Orkney's maritime history. Most dive skippers build a visit to the museum into their weekly diving itinerary.

SMS BRUMMER
58°53'49.0"N 3°09'12.9"W

REMAINS OF THE SEARCHLIGHT WITH ITS DELICATE IRIS BLADES

Launched in 1915, the Bremse-class light cruiser SMS *Brummer* was built for mine-laying with a clear emphasis on velocity. Able to reach speeds of up to 28 knots, her design resembled the Aurora-class of British cruisers due to her curved bow and collapsible main mast. Her light construction has seen her suffer far worse than many of the other wrecks in Scapa Flow with her scythe-like bow providing the starkest example of her rapid decay. Despite this, the *Brummer* still makes for a superb dive.

One hundred years on from her sinking, the wreck lies on her starboard side at a maximum depth of 36m with her bow pointing to the north-west. The top of the *Brummer* is only 22m, making her a perfect multi-level dive. Most divers start their exploration by descending the shotline tied off forward of her bridge. Later in the diving season when viz is at its best, it's worth looking down onto the wreck as you descend the shotline — the sight of the bow stretching out before you can be quite impressive!

Start your dive by exploring the bridge and the distinctive framework structure that once supported it. Unique to the *Brummer*, the viewing platform on the roof of the bridge still has its brass railings in place and is a haven for feather starfish, dead man's fingers and colourful tunicates. Although much of the bridge has collapsed and sunk into the seabed, it's still easy to make out its former shape. On the bottom near the bridge you'll find one of the *Brummer*'s signature features — the remains of a large searchlight. Long since separated from the ship, its outer casing has corroded away completely, revealing the ornate copper iris blades within. Care must be taken to not touch any part of the searchlight as it is extremely delicate.

Heading towards the bow, you'll encounter the armoured command tower with its distinctive thin viewing slits and range finder beneath the peeled away deck. Forward still, you'll find the first of the *Brummer*'s four pedestal-mounted 5.9-inch deck guns along the ship's centre line. A further two of her large calibre guns can be found at her stern arranged in line as a superfiring pair with the remaining one aft of the conning tower.

Heading back past midships, the wreck takes on a far more irregular shape as you reach the area torn open by salvage operations. Almost half the wreckage is now twisted and broken, reflecting the extensive work that took place to recover valuable metals within her engine rooms and her brass torpedo tubes. Keep your eyes open for other visitors around this area — it's not unusual to see the occasional seal playfully exploring the wreck.

The stern is heavily broken up. With much of the superstructure falling away, it is easy to miss the two rear 5.9-inch guns buried underneath. Look for the kedge anchor, still in place. Swim up over the rudder and you'll find a large hole giving access to the steering gear and prop shaft.

Sixty minutes from Stromness by boat. Lies in a north-westerly direction, north of the island of Cava.

BRASS HANDRAIL ON THE BRIDGE

DISTINCTIVE BOW

22–36m

SMS CÖLN
58°53'50.2"N 3°08'31.0"W

5.9" BREACH-LOADING GUN

CAVERNOUS INNER SECTIONS

The German light cruiser SMS *Cöln* was the lead ship of her class, sharing her design and layout with sister ship SMS *Dresden*. Commissioned into the Imperial Germany Navy in January 1918, she joined the Second Scouting Group and enjoyed an uneventful career harassing British convoys in the North Sea.

Located approximately one mile from the *Dresden* with her bow pointing in a north-westerly direction, she's faired far better than her sister and is undoubtedly the most complete of the four cruisers. Whilst she is showing signs of deterioration, the *Cöln* most closely matches the popular perception of a shipwreck. Lying on her starboard side at a depth of 36m with her highest point rising to just 22m below the surface, diving the *Cöln* is a real highlight.

In common with the other Scapa wrecks, salvage operations have taken their toll, with her stern all but separated from the main body of the ship about two-thirds of the way along. Despite this, the stern is worth a visit if only to take in the spectacle of the two super-firing 5.9-inch breach-loading guns pointing ominously out into the gloom. Interestingly, the forward 5.9-inchers near the bow were salvaged — all that remains is the stub of their mounting shaft.

More experienced divers will enjoy the open swim-throughs in the forward section of the hull just before the bridge. Rise up and follow the outer edge of the hull and take in the spectacle of the ship's beautiful vertical deck dropping to the seabed below. Further along you'll encounter a number of holes allowing access to the inner sections of the wreck. A good torch is a must and I strongly recommended you keep a look out for exit points along the way. Inside the wreck you'll see a number of interesting features including the inner workings of the deck-mounted capstans.

Like the *Dresden*, the *Cöln*'s bridge and conning tower may look separate but canvas framework would have surrounded both. Look closely and you'll see one of the ship's guns sticking out of the bridge after being violently forced through as she sank. In the same area you'll find the armoured conning tower with its radar-like range finder still in place. Note the lack of optics — these were removed from all vessels before internment to stop the British from getting them.

Swimming aft from the bridge section, look up towards the top line of the wreck and you'll see another of the *Cöln*'s signature features — a pair of overhanging lifeboat davits still in place. Richly covered in marine growth, these beautiful curved arms extend out from the body of the wreck like massive ribs.

Just before the salvage break, you'll find one of the ship's remaining high-angle 3.7-inch AA guns. Next to it a torpedo tube is oriented with its opening towards the seabed. A much sought-after item, one can only assume it was overlooked during salvage operations.

Sixty minutes from Stromness by boat. Lies in a north-westerly direction, north-east of the island of Cava.

22–36m

CONNING TOWER RANGE FINDER

STERN ANCHOR

SMS DRESDEN
58°52'55.6"N 3°08'23.7"W

SHIELD ON THE BOW

15CM GUN BREACH MECHANISM

A favourite "shake down dive" amongst boat skippers, for many the light cruiser SMS *Dresden* is their first experience of diving the wrecks of the High Seas Fleet. Built in the latter stages of World War I, the *Dresden* is of the same class as the SMS *Cöln* and shares the seabed with her near the island of Cava. Originally built as a light cruiser, she was assigned to the Second Scouting Group and saw action patrolling the North Sea.

Today the wreck lies on her port side with a 40 degree tilt past the horizontal on a gradual slope. Her stern lies at the deepest point of 38m and her bow at 25m. For divers wishing to maximise dive time by staying a little shallower, the wreck rises to a depth of just 17m from the surface above the bridge section. She's generously festooned in a rich covering of marine growth, including colourful sponges and anemones.

Like many German Navy vessels launched in the latter years of the war, the *Dresden* was built using inferior materials compared to ships constructed before the conflict. This is good news for divers as salvage operations were restricted to the more profitable areas of the wreck above the engine room. Only her upper starboard condensers and pumps were removed through blasting, leaving the remaining sections of the hull untouched.

Her lower build quality sadly contributed to her deterioration, however, with large sections of the wreck degrading far quicker than her pre-war counterparts. This is most noticeable at the bow where a large section of the foredeck has succumbed to gravity, peeling away from the hull. Now hanging down so low that it reaches near seabed level, this separation enables a glimpse inside the forward section of the wreck. Peer in with a good torch and you'll see rooms, passageways and ladders previously hidden from view.

Rising above this collapsed section of the bow, look out for her signature feature — an identifying shield that once bore the colourful coat of arms of the City of Dresden. Whilst the colours may have long since faded, the shield itself can still be seen raised up from the hull.

Moving aft of the bridge, you'll encounter the area of the boilers. Of all the light cruisers, the *Dresden* offers the best opportunity to view the inner boiler room workings without the need for penetration. You'll see large amounts of coal strewn across the seabed and look out too for the fire bricks complete with distinctive "KMS" markings that once lined the boiler housings.

There are guns along the full length of the wreck with some of the best examples located near the stern. Here you'll find two of eight large 5.9-inch guns, one of which is still attached whilst the second now lies on the seabed. The shallower of these two guns makes for a great photo opportunity.

- Best avoided during strong northerly winds.

- Sixty minutes from Stromness by boat. Lies half way between the island of Cava and a small rocky island skerry called the Barrel of Butter.

17–36m

CAPSTAN

FIRE BRICKS MARKED WITH "KMS"

SMS KARLSRUHE
58°53'21.7"N 3°11'24.5"W

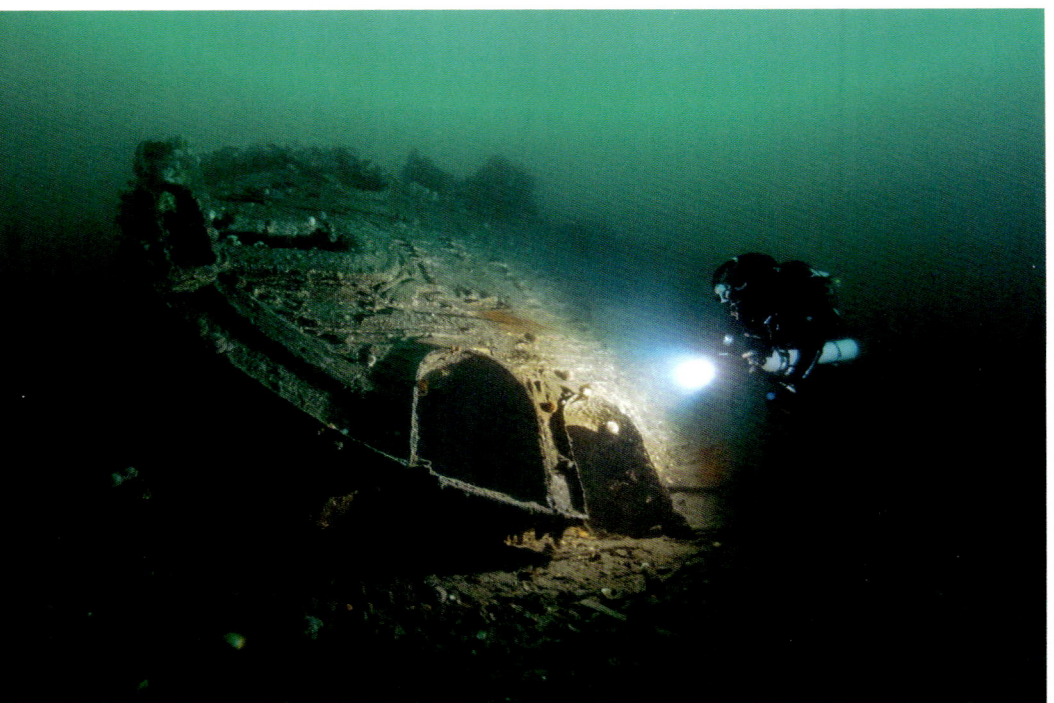

SCALLOPED CUT OUTS AT THE STERN

The SMS *Karlsruhe* is a deceptive wreck. As one of the more heavily deteriorated High Seas Fleet vessels, you'd be forgiven for thinking that she is a less interesting dive than the other more intact German ships in the area. Don't let her state of disarray put you off — she provides a unique opportunity to see aspects of construction and design that are well hidden within the more complete wrecks.

The *Karlsruhe* was a light cruiser of the Königsberg class that entered service with the Imperial German Navy in November 1916. Although similar in size to the *Brummer*, she was more heavily armed, with twice the number of 5.9-inch guns, a pair of 3.7-inch guns and four 20-inch torpedo tubes. Her valuable brass tubes were removed during salvage operations, but the *Karlsruhe* provides some of the better opportunities to see the big guns still in situ. Her collapsed state and 45 degree tilt has opened the wreck up to ambient light too, making her one of the best wrecks for underwater photographers wanting to get that illusive big gun photo.

The *Karlsruhe* benefits from being the shallowest of all the German wrecks. Lying on her starboard side in 27m of water, she rises up to just 14m below the surface. Dropping down one of the shotlines attached at either end of the wreck, her shallow depth and high ambient light levels afford a great view of the wreck below you.

Navigating along the *Karlsruhe* can be disorientating with salvage work having reduced her to a sloping jumble of twisted metal and debris. Starting your dive on the bow shotline, look out for a pair of large capstans lying together — the decking that once supported them has long-since collapsed and peeled open to reveal three lower levels and the worm drive for the capstan winch. The foredeck 5.9-inch guns have fallen on top of each other too.

The remains of the fire control station can still be seen and a hole in the roof where the range finger would have been mounted provides a convenient window to peer inside through. Whilst the bridge has been almost completely salvaged, look down towards the seabed and you'll see the foremast which now lies across the barrel of one of the 5.9-inch guns. This area makes for a great photo opportunity.

No visit to the *Karlsruhe* is complete without a swim around the impressive stern. Although the upper section has deteriorated it continues to be a magnet for photographers. Featuring beautiful teak decking, it's hard to ignore the unique scalloped cut outs on either side. Although their exact purpose is still a mystery, common belief is that they were used to deploy a curtain of smoke behind the vessel.

🕒 Avoid in strong westerly winds.

📍 Sixty minutes from Stromness by boat. Lies facing north-west off the north-westerly tip of the Calf of Cava.

TURBINE CASING

BIG GUNS

ANCHOR CAPSTANS

14–27m

SMS KÖNIG
58°53'10.9"N 3°09'07.9"W

12" THICK CITADEL WALL

LOW-PRESSURE TURBINE

The battleship SMS *König* was the lead ship of her class and saw action at the Battle of Jutland — one of the most important and controversial naval engagements of World War I. On the 31 May 1916, the Imperial German Navy engaged the might of the Royal Navy's Grand Fleet off Denmark's North Sea coast, the outcome of which is still deeply contested to this day. As the lead ship of the 3rd Battle Squadron, *König* held her own despite enduring a number of punishing heavy calibre hits from Admiral Jellicoe's flagship, HMS *Iron Duke*.

Today the wreck of SMS *König* lies in 40m of water east of the island of Cava. Like her sister ships *Kronprinz Wilhelm* and *Markgraf*, the sheer weight of her superstructure caused her to turn turtle as she sank, with the wreck now all but upside down on the seabed. Extensive salvage operations carried out in the 1960s and 70s have proven useful to divers, opening up areas of the wreck not accessible on the other two König-class battleships in the Flow.

Dropping down the shotline, you'll arrive roughly aft of midships at a depth of about 20m. Covering the entire wreck takes at least two good dives so it pays to pick your route carefully. I find the aft section of the wreck to be the more interesting dive, so head towards the stern along the starboard side with the wreck on your left shoulder. Running along the outer hull, you'll see evidence of salvage where large sections of her 14-inch armoured belt has been removed.

Although the stern has suffered substantial damage from blasting, the remains of one of her two rudders still stands up from the hull. Heading forward,

BASE OF THE D-TURRET BARBETTE

the hull rises sharply and you'll enter areas torn open by salvage. Keep an eye open for the 12-inch thick walls of the armoured citadel — this wall of solid steel is just one edge of the armoured "box" within the vessel that provided an additional level of protection to the crew and critical systems during the heat of battle.

Continuing along the wreckage, you'll encounter a large, circular hole approximately 2.5m wide. This is the bottom of the barbette for D-turret within which the housing for a pair of massive 12-inch main guns would have been seated. With the wreck upside down, this is sadly as close as you'll get to seeing the *König*'s formidable primary weapons. Her secondary 5.9-inch guns can be found at seabed level on the starboard side should you find yourself near the bow.

Moving aft, look out for the remains of a large low-pressure turbine. Looking not dissimilar to a large jet engine, the König-class had five more such turbines — two were salvaged and the other three remain buried within the wreck. Further along at the shallowest point you encounter one of the ship's Schulz-Thornycroft boilers. Featuring curved small-bore water pipes running along the full length of the boiler, this distinctive feature is hard to miss.

Sixty minutes from Stromness by boat. Lies facing north-west, east of the Island of Cava

16–40m

SMS KRONPRINZ WILHELM
58°53'36.8"N 3°09'51.9"W

ARMOURED SPOTTING TOWER

The SMS *Kronprinz Wilhelm* was the last of the four König-class dreadnoughts and is all but identical in design to the other two battleships in Scapa Flow. Packing a total of ten 12-inch guns and fourteen 5.9-inch guns ranged along her hull, the *Kronprinz* was a formidable weapon of naval warfare. Like her sister ships, she saw action at the Battle of Jutland and was also involved in the mutiny that broke out aboard several German Navy vessels shortly before the armistice.

Named after the Kaiser's son, the *Kronprinz Wilhelm* now lies north-west of the island of Cava at a maximum depth of 38m. Rising up to just 12m below the surface, she's the most accessible of the three German battleships in Scapa Flow. What makes her so special is her 12-inch guns, which are all but hidden on the other two battleships. The *Kronprinz* has settled on the seabed with a list to starboard leaving her two aft-most turrets exposed.

The shotline on the *Kronprinz* will bring you down on top of the wreck, almost in line with the turrets below. Drop down over the port side of the hull to the seabed and — whilst keeping the wreck on your right shoulder — move towards the stern. Keep your eyes open for a raised area of the deck and move under it. With luck, you should encounter your first gun barrel. Running parallel to the seabed, this is one of the two monstrous 12-inch guns of D-turret.

Continuing aft with the teak deck above you, you'll see the breath-taking spectacle of the aft-most gun turret. Both barrels of E-turret can be seen although their muzzles were forced into the afterdeck as the stern collapsed ahead of them. It's fair to say that it pays to be the first divers to visit this area. Care must be taken not to make contact with the seabed — exiting this area through a cloud of silt will make you very unpopular with any divers unlucky enough to follow.

At this point I normally turn and head in the direction of the bow. Rising up about 4m from the seabed and following the line of the wreck you'll encounter a number of single-barrelled 5.9-inch casemate guns. Seven of these lined the upper deck on each side of the ship.

Continuing along the side of the wreck towards the bow, keep an eye out below for another feature you cannot afford to miss. Drop down onto the seabed and follow what remains of the mast along to the spotting top and take a look inside it through the open roof. This triangular-shaped armoured observation platform with its viewing slits was accessed via a ladder that ran up the inside of the mast. With the outer skin of the mast now heavily corroded, it's possible to see this ladder in situ.

Sixty minutes from Stromness by boat. Lies facing in a north-west direction, east of the Island of Cava.

12–38m

12" GUN LYING FLAT ON THE SEABED

A RICH CARPET OF MARINE GROWTH

SMS MARKGRAF
58°53'29.0"N 3°09'55.5"W

THREE METRE HIGH TWIN RUDDERS

Ask any seasoned Scapa diver what draws them back time and again and you are likely to get the same answer — "The Markgraf". For many visitors, this König-class battleship is without doubt the star attraction. As one of the "big kahunas" of the Kaiser's Navy, the *Markgraf* saw action in many of the war's most famous naval operations including the Battle of Jutland.

Of the three dreadnoughts in the Flow, she has suffered the least salvage damage, with key features like her impressive twin rudders still in place. She lies almost completely upside down at a maximum depth of 42m and her shallowest point at 22m, making her the deepest of the Scapa wrecks. Whilst she favours divers who are willing to incur a little decompression, the *Markgraf* still has plenty to offer single-tank recreational divers.

The wreck normally has two shotlines — one tied at the stern just forward of her rudders and another near the bow on the anchor chain which is wrapped across the wreck. The forward line is always easy to find as the anchor chain runs down to the seabed on the starboard side of the wreck. Located closer to Cava than the other wrecks (with the exception of the *Karlsruhe*), *Markgraf* is more affected by the tide so which shotline you descend will be dependent on the direction of any water flow.

If you only get one dive on her, I recommend dropping down the aft shotline and heading towards the stern to take in what is undoubtedly one of the signature views of Scapa Flow — the massive 3m tall rudders standing proud and in line after more than 100 years underwater. Swimming between them gives a real sense of just how monstrous in size the *Markgraf* really is.

Heading back along the wreck, you can choose one of two routes. Head up past the A-frames that once held the ship's three propellers in place and you'll reach the heavily salvaged area exposing what remains of the ship's turbines and engine room. Alternatively, head down and along the starboard side and you'll encounter a line of 5.9-inch casemate guns and, further on, the forward mast and spotting tower. You'll also see evidence of the removal of large strips of the ship's 12-inch armour plating, which has created a fascinating opportunity to peer deeper inside the ship's hull.

If you get the chance of a second dive, the bow is well worth a visit. It doesn't curve like modern warships but is almost vertical — a perfect example of the classic dreadnought design. Salvage operations have caused the bow section to drop 10m lower than the rest but it's an impressive sight nonetheless. Descending to the seabed and looking up at the bow is a breathtaking experience, especially in good viz.

Roughly north-east of the Calf of Cava, facing north-west. Sixty minutes from Stromness.

22–43m

THE STUNNING BOW

PROPELLER A-FRAME

FACT FILE

GETTING THERE For most visitors, the best way to get to Orkney is via a Northlink Ferry, either from Scrabster at the very tip of the Scottish mainland or from Aberdeen. Most choose the Scrabster route as it's both the cheapest option and will deposit you directly at Stromness. The Aberdeen ferry on the other hand docks in Kirkwall, adding 20 minutes onto your journey and making a bigger dent in your wallet.

ANYTHING ELSE? There is far more to Scapa diving besides the High Seas Fleet. Worth visiting are the 55m-long *James Barrie* (at 43m), the *Tabarka* (15m) — the most beautiful of the three remaining blockships — and the scattered remains of the last German U-boat to be sunk in British waters at the end of World War I, *UB-116* (27m). If you get the opportunity to dive the World War II German escort boat (Corvette), the *F2* (16m), make sure you follow the rope linking it to the nearby *YC21* barge to view the 20mm anti-aircraft guns in its holds.

DIVE OPERATIONS Although we have provided coordinates, diving the German wrecks is only permissible with a permit as they are scheduled ancient monuments. It is also one area in particular where local skippers work extraordinarily hard to ensure that you get the most out of your diving and can relax the rest of the time, not least guiding your wreck choice with regards to the weather. A number of excellent dive boats operate from the Stromness harbourside.
MV Valhalla and MV Valkyrie — www.mv-valkyrie.co.uk
MV Huskyan — www.huskyan.com
MV Clasina — www.mvhalton.co.uk
MV Invincible — www.scapa-flow.co.uk
MV Karin — www.scapaflow.com
MV Jean Elaine — www.jeanelaine.co.uk
Scapa Scuba — www.scapascuba.co.uk (dive shop).

WORLD WAR II ESCORT, THE F2

ORKNEY IS also home to a number of UNESCO World Heritage sites including the Ring of Brodgar and Skara Brae, the remains of a Neolithic settlement older than Stonehenge and the Pyramids. Lying at the same latitude as both southern Greenland and Norway, the archipelago enjoys long, drawn-out summer evenings, giving visitors plenty of time to explore the islands after a day at sea.

Sea temperature is surprising — up to 14 degrees C by late summer — with the North Atlantic current sweeping water up from the Gulf Stream. Whilst there is some limited shore diving, boat diving experience is advisable, as is the ability to deploy a surface marker buoy and ascend in open water if needed. All of the more popular wrecks have fixed shotlines, so there is always the option to ascend those.

Scapa Flow is well served by dive boats, all of which operate from Stromness. Diving here is very different to the rest of the UK with most boat operators working on a six day booking basis — individual days are rarely possible. You'll need to commit to a week on the boat and book well in advance (over a year ahead is not uncommon) as spaces sell out very quickly. Group bookings are popular too.

The good news is that most Scapa boats are "full service", i.e. they safely arrange all the diving, fill your cylinders with whichever funky gas mix you require, and many even provide onboard snacks, meals and drinks. Some operators do this on a liveaboard basis whilst others can arrange accommodation on your behalf in Stromness. Either way, you will spend the night there as all boats return to the harbour at the end of each day's diving.

NEOLITHIC RING OF BRODGAR

SCAPA FLOW MUSEUM, LYNESS

FERRY AND DIVE BOAT MOORED UP

NORTH RONA AND SULA SGEIR

by Kirsty Andrews

It is impossible to cover within the scope of this book all of the diving delights that can be found in the furthest reaches of the United Kingdom. Around and beyond the Outer Hebrides, there are a number of little dots on the map which are magnets for intrepid diving explorers.

Part of the attraction is the sheer remoteness. Sea stacs which above water are visited just by seabirds are the topmost tips of underwater cliffs, arches and caves which are astonishingly vibrant and full of life and colour. Islands which were abandoned decades ago by their human inhabitants are a wonderful refuge for grey seals and every inch of rock underwater is colonised by some living thing.

These islands are of interest to birdwatchers as well as divers, being decreed a National

SULA SGEIR

Nature Reserve in 1956 due to their breeding populations of guillemot, puffin, kittiwake, fulmar and petrel. They are also important locations for grey seals; an estimated 7,500 breed in North Rona and Sula Sgeir every year.

The two sites described here are certainly some of the more difficult to access ones in this book. The easiest method to reach these islands is by liveaboard, ensuring that travel time is used most efficiently. Charter a boat from the mainland and discuss your target sites with your skipper.

With careful planning and lucky conditions it would also be possible to carry out a RIB expedition to North Rona and Sula Sgeir, possibly as an extension to a tour of the Outer Hebrides.

NORTH RONA
59°07'12.0"N 5°49'12.0"W

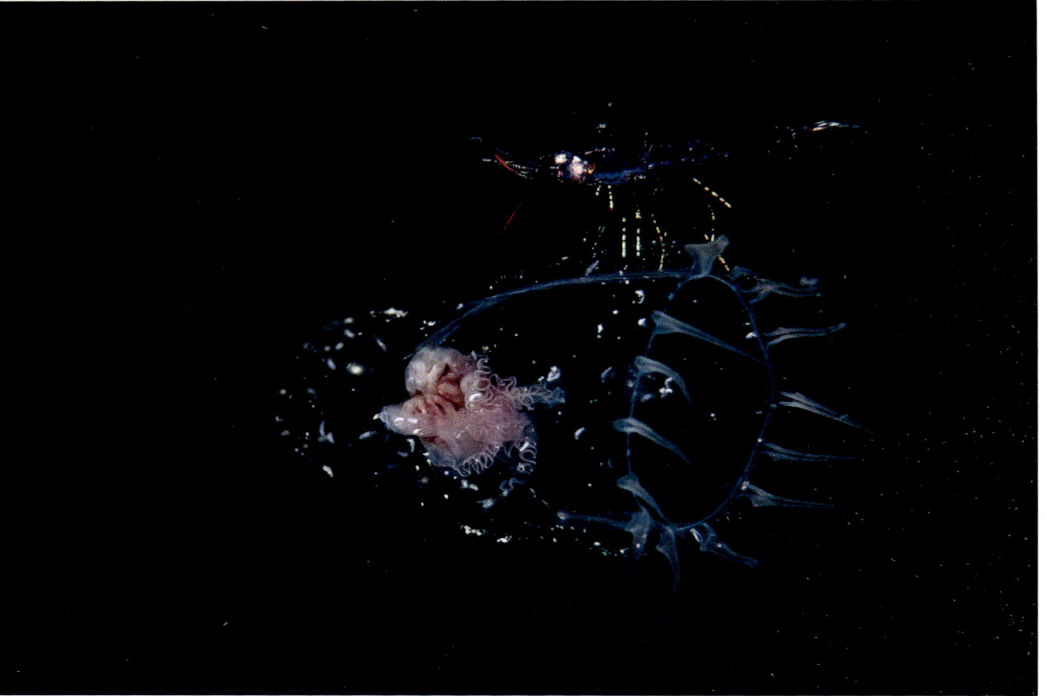

SHRIMP RIDING A COMB JELLY

From above, North Rona is a sloping green island patrolled by fearsome skua and with a steep 108m cliff on one side which shelters puffins and other seabirds. The undulating green turfy moorland is quite a contrast to its bleaker sister, Sula Sgeir, eleven miles away, but Rona is also uninhabited. The island's name is said to come from St Ronan in the eighth century. A rather gruesome tale suggests St Ronan brought his sister Brenhilda to these islands, whose remains were later discovered with a seabird nest inside her ribcage. Others suggest that the name is derived from Old Norse words meaning "rough island". It is called Rona or sometimes North Rona, to differentiate from South Rona, another island in the Hebrides.

Under the waves there are various dive sites to be tried. The topography tends to be a shelving reef, with an initial kelp layer leading to a rocky, bouldery slope, full of dead man's fingers, sponges and anemones, down to approximately 30m where a flat pebbly bottom is covered in brittlestars. Alternatively there are enticing cracks and gullies to be explored with the occasional seal scudding past.

As the waters here are mostly so clear, with regular 20m+ visibility, the kelp layer tends to continue a little deeper than in other, murkier waters. The kelpy shallows and

MONTAGU'S SEA SNAIL

KELP HABITAT

rocky wall are worth a detailed look by eagle-eyed divers for interesting species. You may see various nudibranchs, juvenile fish such as lumpsuckers, scorpionfish and other relatively unusual UK sightings including the Montagu's sea snail (which is actually a fish). Floating on the currents, tiny pteropods flutter past like golden snitches as you start your ascent.

🕒 Slack not required.

📍 Forty-four nautical miles north of the Butt of Lewis, and the same NW of Cape Wrath.

5–30m

NUDIBRANCH (FACELINA AURICULATA)

SULA SGEIR
59°05'37.5"N 6°09'32.0"W

COLOURFUL REEF

The name Sula Sgeir is derived from Old Norse words meaning gannet skerry, or small gannet rock. It is a bare-looking islet without soil or fresh water, beach or landing place. It's a nature reserve but the men of Ness on the Isle of Lewis have permission to harvest young gannets every September, following a long-held tradition. They row over 40 miles north from Lewis to collect the gannets, or guga, and five stone huts remain on Sula Sgeir to house the Nessmen on their hunting trip.

Sula Sgeir is made up of gneiss rock which below water has been transformed by the power of the sea into steep walls and sea caves, including a beautiful arch which runs right through the islet. The visibility tends to be excellent and the water so far from the mainland is an enticing blue. Beyond a short initial kelp layer, every inch of the walls is covered in life, from vibrant orange sponges to a variety of anemones including colourful jewels, dead man's fingers and a host of hydroids.

The wall itself is fabulous but I'd recommend going through the arch as well. The bursting life on the walls continues inside the arch, and clear blue water can be seen at all times. The entrance is at around 27m (don't go too deep or you may miss it) and spirals up to 14m.

As a second dive in this area, the cave complex is worth an explore, and meanders underneath the whole island. Passing through the main entrance at around 15m, initially there is a wide channel that would fit four divers abreast, which leads to a large main chamber at 7–8m with natural light from above. The vibrant turf life on the boulders here reveals that there is plenty of water movement. Other small cracks lead off the main chamber and I was surprised by a couple of grey seals as I explored one of these.

On ascent, look out for hunting seabirds such as guillemots and razorbills, which may well take an interest in your surface marker buoy. Watch out for other interesting creatures passing by — jellyfish, comb jellies, and maybe if you're lucky, sea angels.

A DIVER ENTERS THE ARCH

GUILLEMOT AND RAZORBILL

EXPLORING A CAVE

Slack water is not required.

40 nautical miles north of Lewis.

5–30m

FACT FILE

GETTING THERE Chartering a liveaboard is recommended due to the remote nature of these sites.

ANYTHING ELSE? Usually part of a liveaboard itinerary visiting the north coast of Scotland, the Outer Hebrides and/or St Kilda.

DIVE OPERATIONS Bob at Halton Charters — www.mvhalton.co.uk

NORTH RONA — NUDIBRANCHS ON SEAMAT ON A SNAIL

SULA SGEIR

The author and contributors

WILL APPLEYARD communicates his passion for adventure through his photography and writing. His first two books, *Discover UK Diving* and *Dorset Dives,* became best-sellers and raised awareness of many dive sites. Alongside a string of recreational certifications, Will also holds an HSE commercial media diving qualification. A brand ambassador for O'Three, he is regularly commissioned as photographer and writer for magazines, adventure-based platforms, adventure outfitting and travel brands. In addition to diving, climbing and mountaineering activities have taken him around the world from the glaciers of Iceland to the highest Alpine peaks, the wilds of Canada and to some of the best sport climbing crags in Europe. Skiing and snowboarding top his list of winter activities and when he's not on the mountain, you may find him paragliding over one. www.willappleyard.com

WILL APPLEYARD

KIRSTY ANDREWS has been a diver for over 20 years, in UK waters and beyond. Based in the south-west, she loves the south coast but makes regular pilgrimages to Scotland for the fabulous diving there as well. She writes a monthly column in *SCUBA* and was interviewed about her love of British marine life and excitement in creating photos which show off great UK diving for the BBC's *Blue Planet UK* series. A member of Bristol Underwater Photography Group and the British Society of Underwater Photographers, her photos have been awarded several times in Underwater Photographer of the Year, the British Wildlife Photography Awards and the British Photography Awards. Instagram: @kirstyjandrews

KIRSTY ANDREWS

DAN BOLT Snorkelling and rock pooling as a youngster, Dan learned to dive at 13 and hasn't stopped since. He has an unending fascination with the marine ecosystem and everything it contains, something that still grows to this day. Dan is a regular contributor to *Underwater Photography* magazine and several UK scuba diving magazines. Among other awards, he has twice won the British Underwater Photography Championship and was British Underwater Photographer of the Year 2016. Dan's images regularly feature in the British Wildlife Photography Awards book and the associated travelling exhibition. Dan is a co-founder of, and webmaster to Underwater Photographer of the Year, helping it grow into one of the most respected international underwater photographic competitions. www.underwaterpics.co.uk

DAN BOLT

THE AUTHOR AND CONTRIBUTORS

JASON BROWN What came first, photography or diving? For professional photographer Jason, it's not an easy question to answer. Having learnt to dive back in the 1990s, it didn't take him long to realise that simply being underwater wasn't enough—he also wanted to capture what he saw and share it with a wider audience. From the moment he took his first film camera diving, he was hooked. An accomplished closed-circuit rebreather, technical trimix and cave diver certified through Global Underwater Explorers, Jason takes great pride in capturing eye-catching images that have graced the pages and covers of numerous magazines and other publications around the globe. Whether exploring a shipwreck in cold, green water or pushing deep into a cave, he prides himself on always getting the shot. Whilst he enjoys the lure of warm, clear blue water as much as the next diver, Jason is most at home in the cold, green seas that surround the UK. www.bardophotographic.com

JASON BROWN

JAKE DAVIES grew up on Pen Llŷn, North Wales. Coming from a maritime family, the underwater world played a major role in his life from a young age. A marine biologist, he works as project coordinator for the Angel Shark Project: Wales, which aims to better understand this critically endangered animal. An ambassador for Project Seagrass, Jake raises awareness of the importance of this habitat found off the Welsh coast and assists in field surveys. An HSE Professional Scuba Diver for scientific and media purposes, Jake has been involved with teams filming for the BBC and has supplied footage for Discovery, BBC, ITV and S4C. He dives regularly with the local Llŷn Sub-Aqua Club and during the summer he is either on or under the water exploring and documenting the variety of dive sites along the North Wales coast.
www.jakeddavies1996.wixsite.com/jdscuba

JAKE DAVIES

ALEX GIBSON is the founder and Editor-in-Chief of independent specialist book publisher Dived Up Publications. Since 2013 he has published a range of diving books by expert authors including location guides, underwater photography, maritime history, biography, log books and more. He is an Open Water Instructor and dives regularly with his local British Sub Aqua Club branch (Oxford). A keen underwater photographer, he is a member of the British Society of Underwater Photographers (BSoUP).
www.DivedUp.com

ALEX GIBSON

STUART PHILPOTT began diving in the late 1980s and quickly progressed to instructor level for BSAC, SSI, PADI and TDI training agencies while working at several UK south coast dive centres. Underwater photography became a passion several years later when he had the opportunity to work for a local diving magazine. Over the past 20 years Stuart has seen more than 300 of his articles published, 70 front covers and two books on marine life, dive travel destinations and other underwater activities. His roots are still very much grounded in the UK and he is often seen, camera in hand, at his local dive sites taking pictures throughout the year. adventurediving@yahoo.co.uk. Instagram: @Stuart_Philpott

STUART PHILPOTT

ELAINE WHITEFORD dives all year round in Scotland. She has been diving for 18 years and is qualified as a Master Scuba Diver Trainer. She combined her interests in photography and diving a few years after starting to dive and became a Licentiate of the Royal Photographic Society with a portfolio of underwater images. She has had articles published in a range of magazines and her photographs have been used in a number of books. St Abbs is Elaine's favourite UK destination and she loves the variety of diving in the Philippines. www.sublimescubaphotography.com

ELAINE WHITEFORD